Marital Secrets:
Dating, Lies,
Communication and Sex

Lessons learned by partners in business and marriage with more than 50 combined years of experience in family therapy, social work, psychology, family and divorce law.

Paris M. Finner-Williams, Ph.D., L.P., Esq.
and
Robert D. Williams, MSW, ACSW, DCSW, LMFT

First Edition

RP Publishing
17620 West McNichols Road
Detroit, Michigan 48235
(313) 537-1000

Cover artwork by Alva McNeal

Publisher's Cataloging-in-Publication
(Provided by Quality Books, Inc.)

Finner-Williams, Paris M.
    Marital secrets: dating, lies, communication and sex
 / Paris M. Finner-Williams and Robert D. Williams. —
 1st ed.
    p.cm.
    Includes bibliographical references and index.
    ISBN: 0-9707527-0-9

    1. Man-woman relationships—Religious aspects—Christianity.
2. Marriage—Religious aspects—Christianity. 3. Dating (Social customs). 4. Mate selection. I. Williams, Robert D., 1948- II. Title.

HQ801.F56 2001   646.7'7
                 QBIOl-200321

Printed in the United States of America

This book is dedicated by Paris Michele to

Gerald B. McAdoo, DDS, my uncle who has fostered my academic and professional life, and was the spirited man of God who was the visionary for this book. Thank you for keeping me focused and faithful to the call on my life;

and to

Bernice Finner McAdoo, RN, my beautiful aunt who taught me how to walk as an infant, who eliminates barriers in my path, and who has been the daily wind beneath my wings. Thank you for teaching me how to be a virtuous woman of God by the witness of your Christian life of love, humility, service, biblical study and prayer.

And in loving memory of Fannie Finner, my grandmother and intercessor; Elsie B. Finner Howard, my aunt and caregiver; Iola Finner Mabry, my mother and exhorter; Wayne Edward Finner and William J. Finner, my uncles and protectors; Rev. Hercules Finner, my uncle and spiritual advisor; and all other ancestors who taught me about Jesus, integrity and excellence.

This book is dedicated by Robert Dee to

Trudie Sue Williams, my mother and the late Jessie Williams, my father, who both gave me inspiration and ideas for marriage and family not only by the example of their 57 years of marriage to one another, but also by how they raised 13 children together with pure love, prayer and the Word of God.

Contents

About the Authors vi

Preface viii

Foreword ix

Acknowledgments x

INTRODUCTION: THE MARITAL MISSION OF ROBERT AND
PARIS WILLIAMS 1

CHAPTER ONE: DATING ••••••••••••••••••••••••••••••••••••••• 5

The Family Doughnut: Sweet or Tart Glazing?
The significant impact of the personal and family
histories on the marriage 7
Royal Personalities
The superficial fantasies we hold about our spouse 8
The Dating Derby: Win, Place, or Show
Setting boundaries and guidelines for whom we enjoy,
date or marry 12
Pleasure Dating 14
Investment Dating 15
Finner-Williams Pre-Marital Screening Questionnaire 17
Biblical Courtship 51
Fears of Commitment 51

CHAPTER TWO: LIES 61

*The Wedding Altar Exercise: Unearthing the Golden Vessel
of Problems* 62
Lies We Tell Others: The Different Faces of Infidelity 65
Lies We Tell Ourselves: Fantasies and Faulty Thoughts .. 68
When Givers Marry Sole-Soul Takers
When the investments in marriage don't equal the
returns 69
The Last Straw
Testimonies of plaintiff divorcees 73

CHAPTER THREE: COMMUNICATION 79
Communication, Criticism and Confrontation Styles 80
Chiseling Away at the Spirit 82
Marital Soul-Esteem 86
Twelve Ways Men and Women are Different 89
Eight Ways Husbands Hurt Their Wives 92
Eight Ways Wives Hurt Their Husbands 93

CHAPTER FOUR: SUSTAINING THE RELATIONSHIP 95
Five Signs of a Closed Spirit 96
Six Ways Husbands and Wives Can Open Their Spirits 97
The Breath of Forgiveness 97
Consequences of Unforgiveness 101
Setting Acceptable Relationship Goals 102
Factors for a Successful God-Centered Marriage 108
Techniques for Sustaining Healthy, Stable Romantic
   Relationships 111
The Spiritual Dance of a Man and a Woman 113
The Art of Submission 116
The Marital Mission of Robert and Paris Williams 119

CHAPTER FIVE: SEX 121
Warm Hearts—Cold Beds 121
Male Intimacy 124
Female Intimacy 126
Joy with Menopause 129
Guidelines for Good Sex 132

EPILOGUE: THE LESSON OF THE CACTUS PLANT 135

Appendix: Resources and References 138

Index 140

About the Authors

Dr. Paris M. Finner-Williams, a licensed psychologist and attorney, is the founder and chief executive officer of Detroit, Michigan-based Finner-Williams and Associates Psychological Services, created in 1979. A popular guest on radio and television, she addresses male-female relationship and motivational issues. Her counseling and legal services include these issues as well as family law and probate matters. She is a founder and the first chairperson of the Black African-American Christian Counselors Division of the American Association of Christian Counselors.

Finner-Williams has provided consultation and training to public and private sector agencies and organizations in the areas of group dynamics, client assessment and mental health treatment. She is a member or officer of numerous professional organizations and has received local and national recognition for her contributions and leadership in the mental health field.

Mr. Robert D. Williams serves as executive director of Finner-Williams and Associates Psychological Services and as on-site division manager for a Detroit-based comprehensive community mental health corporation. A licensed marriage and family therapist, he specializes in male-female relationships, child and adolescent concerns and treatment of African-American males. An author of numerous publications and articles, he has appeared on a number of radio and television programs to discuss these issues. With a masters degree in social work, Williams serves as a child custody and divorce mediator, along with his wife.

Mr. Williams has been in clinical practice and mental health administration since 1973. He is a member of or has served on the board of directors for the Academy of Certified Social Workers; the National Association of Black Social Workers; the National Association of Social Workers; and the Association for the Advancement of Social Work with Groups. He also has served as president of the University of Michigan School of Social Workers Alumni Board of Advisors. He is a founder and an advisory board member of the Black African-American Christian Counselors Division of the American Association of Christian Counselors.

Preface

Many couples enter into marriage without asking the right questions or processing the right issues. In times past, parents and other relatives served as role models and sources of information about what healthy marital relationships involve. That information is not readily available now to many dating, engaged and married couples. This work is excellent in raising the kinds of questions and concerns that can make or break a potential or existing relationship. The writers serve as surrogate mothers and fathers—giving out the time-tested advice that is missing today.

I really like how down-to-earth and practical this work is. Many works are so theoretical that they don't match up with what the issues are "on the street." This couple has been in the trenches with many couples and this work reflects this experience.

—Michael R. Lyles, M.D., Psychiatrist
Lyles & Crawford Clinical Consulting, P.C.

Foreword

Marriage often brings together two very different individuals and places them in such close proximity that every flaw and detail will show. The huge challenge for all is "to live joyfully with the one you love all the days of thy vanity" (Ecclesiastes 9:9 NLT). Sadly, most fail. Sixty to seventy percent of those who marry now will wind up going through periods of separation and/or divorce. And these are just statistics. They don't begin to tell the story of those who stay and endure a bad marriage. When our marriages get into trouble...we hurt and the effects of this brokenness go deep.

Why do marriages fail? What about hope, healing and happiness? Dr. Atty. Paris M. Finner-Williams and husband Robert D. Williams love each other, and every day they work feverishly to save and strengthen marriages. We've talked, laughed and shared many stories and thoughts. During those times, I've found a deep love and passion for God in their spirit. I've also found that the Williamses pull no punches. They talk frankly and openly about marital secrets such as masks, anger, infidelity and sexual problems. We need more discussion and direction as we continue to face these challenging and tough issues. May God lead you as you seek "His Ways" in your life, love and ministry.

—Tim Clinton Ed.D., LPC, LMFT
President of the American Association of
Christian Counselors
Author, *Before a Bad Goodbye, The Marriage You've Always Wanted*
Executive Editor of *The Soul Care Bible*

Acknowledgements

Thank you, God, for giving us favor and the presence of the Holy Spirit that has guided us and made possible the birth and completion of this project. To God be the glory!

There are family members who have loved us and nourished our spirits. We want to express our appreciation to the Finner family: Gerald B. McAdoo, II; Vershaun C. Finner; Dr. Rev. N. Thomas Howard; Sidney and Bessie Finner; Earl Murray; Theresa A. Finner-Murray; Rev. Ricardo Bartlett; Tina Finner; Elsie B. Finner; Paul and Audrey Woods; and a host of cousins, aunts and uncles. A special thank you to cousin Dr. Jernice L. McAdoo and aunt Thelma Jean Finner, RN, BSN, MS, for their thoughts and research assistance. We want to thank the Williams family: Curtis Williams, Lula Mae Williams, Rev. Jimmy T. Wafer and wife Angela Wafer, and a host of other brothers, sisters, cousins, aunts and uncles. As the African proverb so aptly says, "We are because they are."

There are extended family members who have embraced us and encouraged us: Patricia Soares; Gloria Truss; Tatum and Mercedes Eason; Sadie Sapp Mahone; Linda Evans; Deborah Meeks Wentum; the Belle Family of Chicago; Dr. William Revely, Jr.; our church family; and the several pastors and ministers who have so graciously allowed us to work with their single members, marital couples and with their marital couples ministries.

We are appreciative of those who have prayed and stood in the gap for us and served as a constant source of support: Ida Smith, David and Kim Peeples; the late Dorothy Pearl Scott; the late Jeanette Mae Louise Millender; and our life-long friends from our high schools; Michigan Rehabilitation Services; the Detroit-Wayne County Community Mental Health System; the American Association of Christian Counselors; the Association of Black Psychologists; the Black African-American Christian Counselors; the National Association of Black Social Workers and the United Conference for Women.

We want to thank those who have served as our technical experts and literary midwives: Rebecca Florence Osaigbovo of Dabar Publishing Company; Gail E. Hicks; Linda Smith; Diane Proctor Reeder; Elaine Rottman; Rev. Estella Brown; Stephanie Love; Cynthia Taueg; Victoria Johnson; Mary Cleveland-Evans; Ericka Ellis; Rev. Rodney Caruthers, II; Atty. Cheryl Belle; Dr. Timothy E. Clinton; Dr. Michael R. Lyles; and Dr. Afi Samella Abdullah.

We are grateful to God for blessing our lives with these and so many other beautiful people.

Imagine a butterfly and its humble, confined life in a cocoon before taking off in flight as one of the world's most beautiful creatures. This self-help book can help a happier you emerge, despite the roads you have traveled or the challenges you face.

Introduction

The Marital Mission of Robert and Paris Williams

The mission of our marriage is to live a quality life together that is based on the Holy Bible and reflective of the personality, spirit and heart of Jesus Christ. It is our intent to enjoy the richness of agape and intimate love daily. The essence of our marriage is to have open, free and honest communications at all times and about all matters that affect our individual and collective, personal and professional lives. We shall view our marriage and our marital home as our refuge and sanctuary from the influences of this world. We shall safeguard the holy bonds of our covenant marriage, pledging that physical separation from each other and divorce shall never be options nor shall they be subjects for discussion. It is our commission to love, honor and respect each other and regard each other as top priorities, second only to our Lord and Savior Jesus Christ. It is our duty to seek mutual agreement on all matters, and to delegate and make assignment of responsibilities based on our individual gifts and motivations. And it is our unified purpose to daily worship and praise the Lord together, to honor God's will and to abide by the biblical requirements for husbands, wives, and marriage.

That is our statement. It took a while for us to get there, though. And we're still not all the way there—but we're enjoying the journey. We'd like to share with you how to start the marriage journey right—and how to enjoy your wedded life.

The goal of this book is to share more than 50 years of combined therapeutic and legal experience by two people who are married to each other. We wish to guide men and women along the journey from dating to marriage in such a way that it will allow them to stretch and grow in their walk of faith. We come to share with you the lessons we have learned from others and from our own experience. We have a commitment to help you transform your life first through self-knowledge, then through self-empowerment.

In no way is this book intended to serve as a substitute for the Holy Bible or for seeking and receiving counseling or therapy from a qualified mental health professional or Christian counselor. We recommend that you study the Word of God and seek such professional services if your situation so indicates.

This book explores the stages of human development from birth through elder status and studies what we have learned from others. We examine how to obliterate barriers and strongholds formed by the needs of the flesh so that men and women can have satisfying relationships spiritually, emotionally and physically. We provide solutions, techniques and approaches that are practical and have proven effective for enhancing romantic relationships among single and married individuals. We hope this book will be a blessing to you and enhance your ability to gain the God-given power, internal light of peace and joy that God intends for your life.

If you are **single**—this book will help you know your potential partner more fully and give you concrete guidelines to determine the advisability of marriage from all standpoints.

If you are **engaged**—this book will help you learn what to expect from marriage and how you both should approach the wedding and your lives together.

If you are **married**—this book will help you learn where you got off track, and what to do to get back on.

This is a self-help book for big boys and girls who are mature enough and strong enough to face, discuss and resolve those intense and serious issues and barriers between men and women in romantic and intimate relationships.

So come and journey with us. We hope you are enlightened by—and enjoy—the ride!

Chapter One:
Dating

How could you?

Why do you say you're going to change but just keep doing the same old thing?

You are not the person I thought I was marrying!
You weren't like this when we were dating!

I should have listened when people told me not to marry you!

Lord, what have I gotten myself into?

If you have said those things, or heard them said to you, congratulations! You have gotten yourself into what we call the institution of marriage—an institution that functions best if each partner acts according to commonly-understood principles. Marriages are unique because individuals are unique; yet, we can discover universal principles that determine the success or failure of couples who enter into this sacred and enduring institution.

Once upon a time, dating and getting married was easy. You met someone from within your community; probably you went to the same schools, the same church. You knew their family and they knew yours. There were few questions. Roles were simple and clear.

How things have changed! The person you meet who may be "the one" may not have grown up in the same area of the country as you. Short of employing a private detective, there may be no way to discover the truth about their family history or background.

What does this mean for dating today? It means that quality relationships will have to include effective communication—a communication which involves going beyond the basic facts to full disclosure, honesty, truth and a sincere commitment to continually improve interactions and understanding.

Who knows? Maybe it's better this way. Marital discord often occurs because during the courtship each spouse fails to complete an *itemized study* of their intended partner. That may sound cold, but it is one reason couples are guarded and are not equipped to resolve the issues in their marriage from a solid position of knowledge, tolerance and acceptance.

An in-depth pre-marital study should be exhaustive, revealing the impact of personal history on each partner's makeup, belief systems and behavior. The history includes, at a minimum, significant life events, family interactions, personality, major life incidents, past traumatic experiences, thoughts, feelings, emotions and behavior, as well as morals, values, beliefs, spirit, soul and faith. A lack of knowledge about your intended will lead to feelings of frustration, anger, bewilderment and a litany of questions like the ones at the beginning of this chapter.

The exhaustive revealing of personal and family histories before the engagement period can provide an explanation for the behavior patterns, thoughts and feelings spouses display *after* the wedding. Full and honest discovery during courtship and dating can reveal a probable answer to the multitude of questions that arise when one is frustrated, angry or bewildered, pondering endlessly a litany of questions and concerns of the heart that often begin with "why did you do that?"

The Family Doughnut: Sweet or Tart Glazing?

> **Dating Secret: When considering a mate, it is important to know who has had the strongest influence on their life.**

As children we first learned how to imitate and emulate immediate and extended family members by observing and interacting with them. We later learned behaviors from our peers and others in our different environments. The family unit is like a glazed doughnut. The "glaze" of the doughnut or home environment may be sweet chocolate, caramel or vanilla; or it may be tart lemon. As we pass back and forth through the powerful and nurturing hole of this imaginary "glazed doughnut," its sweet or tart taste lodges in our mouths, covering our souls and forming our spirits. The shaping of our social learning begins at birth, as we observe the behaviors of others and then attempt them, rehearse them, have them reinforced or punished, and finally repeat or eliminate them in our later lives. Behaviors, potential behaviors and habits often are chosen according to whom we choose to model.

The impact of our personal and family histories will strongly impact the quality of our relationships, the effectiveness of our interpersonal communications and our ability to fully disclose our true selves. How we were "glazed" will determine if we will be honest, truthful, sincere and faithfully committed. The way we were "glazed" affects the quality of our thoughts, the stability of our emotions and the normality of our feelings. The way we were "glazed" will affect our level of trust, independence and ability to change. It will determine our work ethic and our experience of shame, guilt, or doubt. The way we were "glazed" will influence whether we feel inferior or have a strong ego. It will guide us to experience role confusion or the ability to demonstrate appropriate intimacy, to hope or despair, to community or isolation.

If we are "glazed" sweetly, we will have hope, steadfastness, willpower, purpose, mission, and competence. If we are "glazed" sweetly we will demonstrate fidelity, faithfulness, a willingness to give and receive love, a caring spirit, wisdom and peace. On the other hand, if we were "glazed" bitterly, we may demonstrate fear, self-doubt, insecurity, inadequacies, incompetencies, uncertainties, indecisiveness and promiscuity. If we were "glazed" bitterly, we may have selfishness, dissatisfaction, meaningless living and lack a strong moral core.

> **Dating Secret: Thoroughly and exhaustively know the ingredients, recipe and "glazing" of your intended's "family doughnut."**

Your ability to cope with and accept the issues in your marriage will be determined by how well you can illuminate and expound on your intended partner's personal and family history "glazing." Haven't you ever noticed that people who come from families with histories of long, quality marriages tend to form lasting, lifetime relationships? If you don't know what a good marriage looks like, it is difficult to emulate. You can't do what you haven't been taught.

> **Dating/Marriage Secret: We are what we have touched, witnessed and learned.**

Royal Personalities

In our clinical practice for the past three decades, clients pursuing marriage opportunities have listed several basic traits they desire in a mate. At the wedding altar, often each expects the other to have a regal personality: victorious, honorable in all affairs and a leader in their family, community, and society. This unrealistic image is usually further exaggerated, fantasized and expanded once the marriage vows are exchanged. We have compiled a list of these items over the years, describing them with the phrase, "The Royal Personality":

- Self-controlled
- Self-confident
- A good confidant for others
- Loyal
- Proud
- Spiritually secure
- Trustworthy
- Forgiving
- Indifferent to criticism
- Good reputation
- Good or classic dress style and grooming
- Discreet
- Responsible
- Shows elegance and good taste
- Enjoys close relationships
- Exhibits stable relationships with partner's family members and friends
- Courteous
- Good planner
- Merciful
- Prosperous and fortunate
- Self-empowered
- Assertive
- Authoritative
- Influential with others
- Exhibits social conscience
- Gives generously of self and resources
- Involved in worthwhile human social causes and public service activities
- Respected and reverent
- Devoted
- Hardworking
- Tenderhearted

- Balanced
- Prayerful
- Friendly
- Positive
- Teachable
- Sincere
- Sensitive and compassionate
- Goal directed
- Shows a sense of humor
- Good listener
- Physically attractive
- Christian

It is significant that the party who describes this ideal "king" or "queen" usually has neither demonstrated nor witnessed these traits in their totality. The Word of God reminds us that all have sinned and come short of God's glorious standard (Romans 3:23 NLT). No spouse will demonstrate all of the above traits. But in reality, we have found that the partner usually claims to possess two-thirds to nine-tenths of these traits; and they typically see far fewer of the traits exhibited in the other person. It is inevitable that ultimately they will fall short of the wedding day fantasies they have of each other.

When we are dating and courting, often our eyes are closed to the truth about our intended's shortcomings, and our spirit and heart are open. In contrast, with the mounting intensity of marital problems, our eyes become open to the shortcomings of our spouse, and our spirit and heart become closed.

Marital Secret: As a spouse, work hard to acquire and exhibit the "royal" traits.

It is important to determine what qualities and traits your partner has by observing what they actually and consistently *do*, not what they *say* for 12 to18 months prior to becoming engaged to marry. If you don't like the behavior you see with your eyes then do **not** marry. After you have married, it is important to accept your decision to marry that specific person, staying focused on what is good in the partner instead of what is lacking. Release the ill feelings, disappointment and anger with yourself for marrying someone who does not fit the image of the mate you dreamed about nor who meets your every expectation for a spouse. Get over it; move on and enjoy the true marriage set before you. Pray for change, peacefully establish mutual agreements toward change, and in the meantime be content in the moment. Learn to love the one you consciously chose to marry. Fully accept your own free will decision to marry a person whom you are not pleased with. This higher level of consciousness will make it easier to achieve marital contentment and see your spouse as your refuge and as your home.

> **Dating Secret: When the eyes are closed, the spirit is open; when the eyes are open, the spirit is closed.**

Modern dating, as we know it, has only been observed for about 100 years. Such dating is merely social and recreational and can serve a number of purposes: stress relief, social inter-course, immediate gratification, and sometimes even privileges usually limited to marriage, albeit without the responsibilities. This kind of dating today is characterized by superficial discus-sions about school, jobs, problems in the work place, activities of the week, hobbies and relationships with others. It is only in-frequently that couples involved in this kind of superficial dating will discuss their personal history and struggles, spiritual strong-holds, weaknesses, fears, insecurities, inadequacies and worries. Tragic and irreconcilable marital discord is too often the result of failure to discover this information during the dating stage.

Courtship was **honored** prior to the 21st century; it required a more thorough, in-depth and itemized study of each other and the two families involved. The investigation would allow both individuals to make competent and informed decisions whether to invest in each other and each other's families. The decision to further invest in the person also would involve making a commitment to support that person's intimate walk with their God, a commitment to their purpose and mission in life, and a commitment to the spiritual calling on their life. Such a complete investigation would not be perceived as intrusive, but instead would honor the personal value, relevance and standing that the person held in the life of their beloved. In the biblical model, courtship usually occurs once in a lifetime, and the ultimate goal is a binding life-long covenant marriage. The biblical model of courtship is limited only to those persons viewed as having a "winner" standing.

The Dating Derby: Win, Place, or Show

Dating is something like thoroughbred horse racing, considered by most horse owners and trainers to be the *premier* form of racing. Horse races are full of excitement. The colors, the sounds, the smells and the suspense combine to make palms sweat and hearts race. Some races have high stakes that attract many of the nation's finest horses and therefore increase the wagering, sometimes to an all-time high. While wagering and attendance may remain strong, it often falls after a thoroughbred's initial year of racing.

Faithful racing fans usually maintain their strong support of thoroughbred horses even when they face stiff competition. They appreciate the horse's quality, they like the prestige, and they enjoy the "perks" that go with being supportive fans. The dollars they provide attract top stables and horses.

Breeders raise horses, owners race them, trainers train them, riders ride them and fans bet on them to win. Some horses successfully establish themselves as top grass horses and some have fewer victories. Horses that have been defeated can come back to win over better-known thoroughbreds.

As a spectator and player, it is most important to identify and evaluate each horse, then decide whether you think they will "win," "place," or "show." Each horse race is a test. And each test is a trial intended to ascertain the quality, value or character of each horse. Similarly, the trials of dating test your trust and belief in your date. The trials of dating allow you to ascertain the person's quality, value and character.

I Peter 1:7 tells us about the test of our faith. The trials of dating are to test your faith in the relationship and to demonstrate if the relationship is strong and pure. The dating process is a test, just like fire tests and purifies gold. If your faith in the person remains strong after being tried by the fires of dating, it will bring you much joy, assurance and honor if God reveals that you should marry.

I John 4:1 (NLT) tells us "Dear friends, do not believe everyone who claims to speak by the spirit. You must test them to see if the spirit they have comes from God." Many of you may unknowingly be in a losing situation with the person whom you are dating. But you must understand that it takes a spiritual test—and testimony—to get a winning marital attitude.

In a competitive horse race the third horse to finish is said to occupy the least contest position called "show." Similarly, in the sport of dating a contestant in the "show" position is one whose outward acts, looks and words hold true when subjected to public inspection, tests and social trials. This is the person you have begun to accompany to public functions.

A horse that occupies the second spot at the finish line is said to "place." Dating contestants worthy of the "place" designation usually are best at sharing our physical space at home. We feel relaxed, comfortable, at ease and in harmony with them in our personal surroundings. As in a horse race, some whom we date will come to the post of "place" in our lives. Such persons have successfully completed the spiritual trials of dating and have reached this higher level on our dating scale.

At the ultimate height of any dating scale is the one whom we label a "winner." Winning thoroughbred horses receive the prize purse and occupy the winner's circle at the end of the horse race.

To have a "win in the dating derby one must successfully complete trials that render them praiseworthy. To "win" the spiritual trials of dating one must have exhibited distinguishable ability and hard work.

The "winner" in our life should be the one who has won our admiration, favor and acceptance. The "winner" in our life should be the one who has successfully overcome each spiritual trial in the dating race. The "winner" in our life, just like the winning race horse, should be the one who has arrived at a special status in the relationship and acquired a special spiritual marital attitude toward you. The one whom you marry should be worthy enough to occupy the winner's circle at the end of the dating race.

Let's now look to the kinds of dating that one can engage in. Then you'll be able to decide where your date fits.

Pleasure Dating: Only the Beginning

"Pleasure Dating" occurs in the initial months of the relationship. It cannot sustain over the long-term. In fact, if it does, the inevitable result is trouble.

In the "Pleasure Dating" phase, the individuals are easily excited and aroused by the outward appearance of each other. We far too often rush to judge that a Pleasure Date is "the one." We then tell our friends and relatives exaggerated truths and fantasies about this new "special person." This emotional activity enhances our senses, causing us to become romantically delusional, deaf to the truth, blind to the obvious and racing at full speed toward a wedding altar built on sinking sand. Pleasure Daters often rush toward marriage with inadequate information and without a solid foundation.

If a Pleasure Date's worthiness doesn't increase with time, the superficiality and good facade will wither away after the initial 12 to 18 months of dating.

> **Dating Secret: It is difficult to maintain the appearance of righteousness and sincerity for more than 12 to 18 months.**

One partner involved in the Pleasure Dating phase may be faithful, committed and a strong support of the other person even in the face of competition in the dating race. They will give privileges better limited to a more serious relationship. Unfortunately, this one committed Pleasure Dater may attract others who are better at receiving than giving. Thus, the dating race becomes handicapped to the receiver's advantage.

Before giving out privileges, it is important to discover the answers to questions like: How was this person raised? What would friends, former romantic partners, even former spouses say about this person? Who are their peers, mentors, and intimate friends? Who are the people they aspire to emulate? Are they dating anyone else right now? Do they want to?

And before these questions are answered, it is important to set "revocable boundaries." Some people are great friends to spend time with watching television at home. Others love to go out to restaurants or formal events. Still others are great for sports or fitness activities. However, none of these people will necessarily advance to the "winner" category. Until you spend significant time finding out about a person and their background, it is important not to send the wrong signals to a "place" or "show" dating relationship.

Investment Dating: A Way to Investigate

Typically, after four to six months of Pleasure Dating, you may proceed to "Investment Dating." This is the phase in which the important questions mentioned above begin to be answered in more detail.

Here's a tool that can help. The Finner-Williams Pre-Marital Screening Questionnaire (PMSQ) is made up of more than 100 questions that let you know how familiar you are with your partner. The questions are based on a combined total of more than 50 years of counseling and legal experience. We questioned numerous individuals about what it was they failed to know about their partner or spouse which led to marital discord, separation, and/or divorce.

It may be beneficial to re-take this screening test every three to four months, after an initial three months of dating, to determine if you are getting better acquainted with each other or becoming stagnant in the Pleasure Dating stage. If you answer it honestly, you will know whether you are "Pleasure Dating," "Investment Dating," or in the phase we call "Biblical Courtship" (to be explained later).

By now you may be saying, "How unromantic, crude and impersonal!" To you we say, "So is divorce." This screening survey will assist you with determining whether you know enough about the person you are considering marrying and whether you can accept their issues and inadequacies.

> **Marital Secret: Do not rush to conclusions about the relevancy that a dating partner should have in your life. Observe a person's behavior throughout the four seasons to learn how they handle a full array of life circumstances.**

THE FINNER-WILLIAMS PRE-MARITAL SCREENING QUESTIONNAIRE

INSTRUCTIONS: This questionnaire consists of six groups of statements. Please read each group of statements carefully. Find your Full Disclosure and Acceptance (FDAA) Score by following the simple mathematical procedures at the end of the questionnaire. The FDAA total score is the sum of the ratings given in boxes A, B, and C on all 150 items. There are six sub-total scores for A, B, and C that are totaled at the end.

FIRST STEP: Box A—Indicate if you had an **opportunity to observe** or learn this item/behavior/personal data about the person.

Write "0" if there is **no knowledge** at all.
Write "1" if there is **some degree of knowledge** or if this item is **not applicable** to the other person.

SECOND STEP: Box B—Indicate to what **degree you have knowledge** about this item/behavior/personal data about the other person.

Write "0" if there is **no knowledge at all** or a very slight amount.
Write "1" if there is a **little** amount of knowledge.
Write "2" if there is an **average** amount of knowledge.
Write "3" if there is **complete** knowledge known or if this item is not applicable to the other person.

THIRD STEP: Box C—Indicate to what degree each of the following items/behaviors/information **is acceptable** to you with no anticipation of change for the next 50-70 years.

Write "0" if it is **not acceptable**, you can barely stand it and the other person must change it as soon as possible.

Write "1" if it is **very unpleasant**, but you could stand it with no anticipation of a change.

Write "2" if it **does not bother you much**, and you can accept it with no anticipation of a change.

Write "3" if it is **completely acceptable** with no anticipation of a change, or it is **not applicable** to the other person.

This screening process is intended to be used when someone has determined that their partner is a "Winner." *The time frames associated with the various topics are advisory, flexible and informal guidelines.* The order in which one may consider the following questions should be determined by what issues are most important to the individual who is engaged in the Investment Dating process. Feel free to use your own personal language and words if necessary, as long as they parallel the concepts listed. It is our professional opinion and personal belief that, in most situations, a couple should date a minimum of 12 to 18 months *before* discussing the possibility of becoming engaged to marry. Also, it is our contention that if you do not know and accept the answers to a majority of the following questions and their sub-parts, then it is not time to become engaged and/or married. Try to cover at least two to three areas each month. May God bless you with wisdom, discernment, self-empowerment, grace, compassion and mercy as you undertake this journey.

1-3 **Months** **of Dating**	**A: Degree of Observation** 0=**no knowledge** 1=**some degree of knowledge** or this item is **not applicable** to this person	**B: Degree of Knowledge** 0=**not at all** or very slightly 1=a **little** knowledge 2=an **average** knowledge 3=**complete** knowledge or this item is **not applicable**	**C=Degree of Acceptance** 0=**not acceptable** 1=**very unpleasant** 2=**does not bother you much** 3=**completely acceptable** or not applicable
Do you know the full name of the person you have been dating?			
Have they ever been known by any other name(s)?			
What history does the person have of physical, medical, mental and emotional problems; developmental delays; allergies; learning disorders; alcohol or substance abuse?			
On a typical day, how much do they use alcohol, marijuana, cocaine, heroin and/or cigarettes?			
How much education did they complete?			

1-3 MONTHS OF DATING	A: Degree of Observation 0=no knowledge 1=some degree of knowledge or this item is **not applicable** to this person	B: Degree of Knowledge 0=**not at all** or very slightly 1=a **little** knowledge 2=an **average** knowledge 3=**complete** knowledge or this item is **not** applicable	C=Degree of Acceptance 0=**not acceptable** 1=**very unpleasant** 2=**does not bother you much** 3=**completely acceptable** or not applicable
When did they earn their high school diploma or GED?			
How many college/ community college years/credits do they have?			
What is/was their college major?			
What is/was their GPA?			
Why did they drop out of school/college?			
When attending school, were they in regular classes or special education classes?			
How many times were they suspended in school and for what reasons?			
Have they ever been married before?			

1-3 MONTHS OF DATING	A: Degree of Observation 0=no knowledge 1=some degree of knowledge or this item is not applicable to this person	B: Degree of Knowledge 0=not at all or very slightly 1=a little knowledge 2=an average knowledge 3=complete knowledge or this item is not applicable	C=Degree of Acceptance 0=not acceptable 1=very unpleasant 2=does not bother you much 3=completely acceptable or not applicable
How many times?			
What is their current marital status?			
How many sons, daughters, foster children, step-sons, adopted sons, step-daughters and/or adopted daughters do they have?			
How did their former spouse contribute to the failure of their marriage(s)?			
How did they personally contribute to the failure of their own marriage(s)?			
Have they ever been in the military service?			
If so, what branch of the military?			

1-3 MONTHS OF DATING	A: Degree of Observation 0=no knowledge 1=some degree of knowledge or this item is **not applicable** to this person	B: Degree of Knowledge 0=**not at all** or very slightly 1=a **little** knowledge 2=an **average** knowledge 3=**complete** knowledge or this item is **not applicable**	C=Degree of Acceptance 0=**not acceptable** 1=**very unpleasant** 2=**does not bother you much** 3=**completely acceptable** or not applicable
When were they discharged from the military?			
Are they in the military reserves?			
What was their military rank at discharge?			
What was their military discharge status?			
What educational experiences did the person's parents receive?			
What are/were the occupations of the person's parents?			
How old were the person's parents when he or she was born?			

1-3 MONTHS OF DATING	A: Degree of Observation 0=no knowledge 1=some degree of knowledge or this item is not applicable to this person	B: Degree of Knowledge 0=not at all or very slightly 1=a little knowledge 2=an average knowledge 3=complete knowledge or this item is not applicable	C=Degree of Acceptance 0=not acceptable 1=very unpleasant 2=does not bother you much 3=completely acceptable or not applicable
What is the ethnic background of their parents and maternal/paternal grandparents?			
Is the person homosexual, heterosexual or bisexual?			
What is the quality of their dress style, grooming skill, personal appearance and personal/oral hygiene?			
Sub-total for months 1-3 (30 items): A # _____ B # _____ C # _____			

4-6 MONTHS OF DATING	A: Degree of Observation 0=no knowledge 1=some degree of knowledge or this item is not applicable to this person	B: Degree of Knowledge 0=not at all or very slightly 1=a little knowledge 2=an average knowledge 3=complete knowledge or this item is not applicable	C=Degree of Acceptance 0=not acceptable 1=very unpleasant 2=does not bother you much 3=completely acceptable or not applicable
Whom does the person live with and is this permanent?			
How clean do/did their parents keep their home(s)?			
How many times have they been held at the juvenile detention facility, local police precinct, booked into a county jail, or incarcerated in prison?			
What were the charges for each?			
Are they currently on probation or parole, and if yes, when does it expire?			
Do they own their house or do they rent?			

4-6 MONTHS OF DATING	A: Degree of Observation 0=no knowledge 1=some degree of knowledge or this item is not applicable to this person	B: Degree of Knowledge 0=not at all or very slightly 1=a little knowledge 2=an average knowledge 3=complete knowledge or this item is not applicable	C=Degree of Acceptance 0=not acceptable 1=very unpleasant 2=does not bother you much 3=completely acceptable or not applicable
How clean do they keep their home?			
Do you like the way that they talk to you?			
What is their religion and faith?			
Where do they worship and how often, in which ministries are they actively involved, and what spiritual gifts do they recognize in themselves?			
Are they saved and what do they understand to be the plan of salvation?			
What is their purpose (i.e., goal, aim, desire, intention) in life?			
Are they happy and how does their happiness show?			

4-6 MONTHS OF DATING	A: Degree of Observation 0=no knowledge 1=some degree of knowledge or this item is not applicable to this person	B: Degree of Knowledge 0=not at all or very slightly 1=a little knowledge 2=an average knowledge 3=complete knowledge or this item is not applicable	C=Degree of Acceptance 0=not acceptable 1=very unpleasant 2=does not bother you much 3=completely acceptable or not applicable
What is their mission (i.e., self-imposed duty or God-imposed will) in life?			
What do they sense is the difference between God's voice and their personal desires and direction?			
How many happily married friends do they have, and how many of them have been married at least ten years?			
What are their views on abortion?			
What is the overall nature of their current relationship with their mother, father, all grandparents, maternal siblings, paternal siblings, biological siblings, aunts, uncles, and cousins?			

4-6 MONTHS OF DATING	A: Degree of Observation 0=no knowledge 1=some degree of knowledge or this item is not applicable to this person	B: Degree of Knowledge 0=not at all or very slightly 1=a little knowledge 2=an average knowledge 3=complete knowledge or this item is not applicable	C=Degree of Acceptance 0=not acceptable 1=very unpleasant 2=does not bother you much 3=completely acceptable or not applicable
How many single people are in their family?			
What is the overall nature of their current relationship with their neighbors, co-workers, supervisors at work, teachers, classmates, friends and others?			
Sub-total for months 4-6 (20 items): A # _____ B # _____ C # _____			

7-9 MONTHS OF DATING	A: Degree of Observation 0=no knowledge 1=some degree of knowledge or this item is not applicable to this person	B: Degree of Knowledge 0=not at all or very slightly 1=a little knowledge 2=an average knowledge 3=complete knowledge or this item is not applicable	C=Degree of Acceptance 0=not acceptable 1=very unpleasant 2=does not bother you much 3=completely acceptable or not applicable
What is the person's birthday, place of birth and birth hospital?			
Were there any problems during their mother's pregnancy or delivery?			
Was the person adopted?			
How often do they wash dishes, wash clothes, iron clothes, vacuum, dust, mop, etc. each week?			
What type of housekeeper do people say they are?			
Is the title to their automobile in their name?			
Do they have a valid driver's license?			

7-9 MONTHS OF DATING	A: Degree of Observation 0=no knowledge 1=some degree of knowledge or this item is not applicable to this person	B: Degree of Knowledge 0=not at all or very slightly 1=a little knowledge 2=an average knowledge 3=complete knowledge or this item is not applicable	C=Degree of Acceptance 0=not acceptable 1=very unpleasant 2=does not bother you much 3=completely acceptable or not applicable
Do they have any outstanding tickets or warrants?			
Have they ever been violent, abusive, or hit someone?			
If yes, what happened? When was the first time? How frequent was it?			
When was the last time it happened?			
Have they shown signs of jealousy or control?			
What licenses and certifications do they have?			
What is the longest job they ever held?			
How many jobs have they had in the past ten years?			

7-9 MONTHS OF DATING	A: Degree of Observation 0=no knowledge 1=some degree of knowledge or this item is not applicable to this person	B: Degree of Knowledge 0=not at all or very slightly 1=a little knowledge 2=an average knowledge 3=complete knowledge or this item is not applicable	C=Degree of Acceptance 0=not acceptable 1=very unpleasant 2=does not bother you much 3=completely acceptable or not applicable
What current problems are they experiencing with their job?			
What barriers to gainful employment do they perceive that they have?			
What positive employable factors do they possess?			
Where do they work now?			
What positions have they held for the past ten years?			
Have they undergone any gender/ sex organ reassignment surgeries?			
How comfortable are they with discussing sex?			

7-9 MONTHS OF DATING	A: Degree of Observation 0=no knowledge 1=some degree of knowledge or this item is not applicable to this person	B: Degree of Knowledge 0=not at all or very slightly 1=a little knowledge 2=an average knowledge 3=complete knowledge or this item is not applicable	C=Degree of Acceptance 0=not acceptable 1=very unpleasant 2=does not bother you much 3=completely acceptable or not applicable
Are they sexually active?			
If yes, what are their sexual activities?			
Are they a virgin?			
Have they ever engaged in homosexual, incestuous (sexual activity with family members), or pedophilic (sexual activity with children) activities— either as an adult or as a child?			
What is their religious belief about pre-martial sex and sex within the bonds of marriage?			

7-9 MONTHS OF DATING	A: Degree of Observation 0=no knowledge 1=some degree of knowledge or this item is not applicable to this person	B: Degree of Knowledge 0=not at all or very slightly 1=a little knowledge 2=an average knowledge 3=complete knowledge or this item is not applicable	C=Degree of Acceptance 0=not acceptable 1=very unpleasant 2=does not bother you much 3=completely acceptable or not applicable
What is their ability to (1) keep promises, (2) be trustworthy, (3) admire, honor and respect their spouse, (4) enjoy the company of their spouse, and (5) enjoy other's company with their spouse?			
What is their ability to (1) accept constructive criticism, (2) maintain a positive mood, and (3) consistently express rational and logical thoughts when they are at peace, upset or angry?			
Sub-total for months 7-9 (29 items): **A #** _____ **B #** _____ **C #** _____			

10-12 MONTHS OF DATING	A: Degree of Observation 0=no knowledge 1=some degree of knowledge or this item is not applicable to this person	B: Degree of Knowledge 0=not at all or very slightly 1=a little knowledge 2=an average knowledge 3=complete knowledge or this item is not applicable	C=Degree of Acceptance 0=not acceptable 1=very unpleasant 2=does not bother you much 3=completely acceptable or not applicable
Who raised the person?			
Where were they raised?			
What were the sleeping arrangements?			
How would the person describe their childhood?			
Were they abused in any way (i.e.; emotional, mental, physical, sexual, etc.) as a child?			
Were they neglected or abandoned as a child?			
How often do they see their biological/adopted/foster children through the week, weekends, major holidays, minor holidays?			

10-12 MONTHS OF DATING	A: Degree of Observation 0=no knowledge 1=some degree of knowledge or this item is not applicable to this person	B: Degree of Knowledge 0=not at all or very slightly 1=a little knowledge 2=an average knowledge 3=complete knowledge or this item is not applicable	C=Degree of Acceptance 0=not acceptable 1=very unpleasant 2=does not bother you much 3=completely acceptable or not applicable
How do they feel about having more children?			
How do they feel about adopting children?			
How do they feel about having foster children?			
How do they feel about having step-children?			
Are they party to active/outstanding paternity court actions?			
Do they have any children or possible paternity court actions that could be brought against them?			
If yes, what are the details about the children and/or possible paternity court actions?			

10-12 MONTHS OF DATING	A: Degree of Observation 0=no knowledge 1=some degree of knowledge or this item is not applicable to this person	B: Degree of Knowledge 0=not at all or very slightly 1=a little knowledge 2=an average knowledge 3=complete knowledge or this item is not applicable	C=Degree of Acceptance 0=not acceptable 1=very unpleasant 2=does not bother you much 3=completely acceptable or not applicable
What is their competency and ability to (1) solve ownership problems, (2) be a reliable source of information, and (3) communicate clearly?			
What is their competency and ability to (1) deal with emergencies, (2) be assertive, (3) argue constructively?			
What is their competency and ability to (1) help solve a school subject and problem with a child, (2) help with everyday medical problems, (3) help a child deal with a bully and (4) show leadership skills?			

10-12 MONTHS OF DATING	A: Degree of Observation 0=no knowledge 1=some degree of knowledge or this item is not applicable to this person	B: Degree of Knowledge 0=not at all or very slightly 1=a little knowledge 2=an average knowledge 3=complete knowledge or this item is not applicable	C=Degree of Acceptance 0=not acceptable 1=very unpleasant 2=does not bother you much 3=completely acceptable or not applicable
Emotionally, how do they reconcile with what people "say" they will do versus what people "actually do" when both behaviors are inconsistent?			
How would they ensure that there would be consistent non-sexual romance in the marriage for an estimated 50-70 years?			
What type of non-sexual romance activity would they expect of you?			
What non-sexual romance activities would they do for you as their spouse?			

10-12 MONTHS OF DATING	A: Degree of Observation 0=no knowledge 1=some degree of knowledge or this item is not applicable to this person	B: Degree of Knowledge 0=not at all or very slightly 1=a little knowledge 2=an average knowledge 3=complete knowledge or this item is not applicable	C=Degree of Acceptance 0=not acceptable 1=very unpleasant 2=does not bother you much 3=completely acceptable or not applicable
Do they foresee that they will need to assume responsibility for the care of a family member in the future (e.g., parents)?			
What would be the daily/regular care options for the family member in need?			
How many divorces have occurred in their family?			
What is the infidelity history of their parents?			
How many couples in their family are still married after 25 years?			
Are these couples in their family happy? If so, how does it show?			

10-12 MONTHS OF DATING	A: Degree of Observation 0=no knowledge 1=some degree of knowledge or this item is not applicable to this person	B: Degree of Knowledge 0=not at all or very slightly 1=a little knowledge 2=an average knowledge 3=complete knowledge or this item is not applicable	C=Degree of Acceptance 0=not acceptable 1=very unpleasant 2=does not bother you much 3=completely acceptable or not applicable
Were either of their parents unfaithful in the marriage (if applicable)?			
What is the person's spirit, quality of thoughts, mood, emotional state, tone of voice, facial expression and interaction when they're happy, sad, stressed or indifferent?			
Sub-total for months 10-12 (29 items): A # _____ B # _____ C # _____			

13-15 MONTHS OF DATING	A: Degree of Observation 0=no knowledge 1=some degree of knowledge or this item is not applicable to this person	B: Degree of Knowledge 0=not at all or very slightly 1=a little knowledge 2=an average knowledge 3=complete knowledge or this item is not applicable	C=Degree of Acceptance 0=not acceptable 1=very unpleasant 2=does not bother you much 3=completely acceptable or not applicable
What medications have they taken or do they take now, and why?			
What antipsychotic or antidepressant medication are they taking now or previously?			
Is another person's name on their financial assets and/or debts, real property or personal property?			
What is their debt status?			
To whom do they owe money?			
How much do they owe to each collector?			
What debts are past due?			
What is their debt elimination plan?			

13-15 MONTHS OF DATING	A: Degree of Observation 0=no knowledge 1=some degree of knowledge or this item is **not applicable** to this person	B: Degree of Knowledge 0=**not at all** or very slightly 1=a **little** knowledge 2=an **average** knowledge 3=**complete** knowledge or this item is **not applicable**	C=Degree of Acceptance 0=**not acceptable** 1=**very unpleasant** 2=**does not bother you much** 3=**completely acceptable** or **not applicable**
Have they ever been sued by a collector or filed for bankruptcy? If so, what was the outcome?			
How much do they owe in child support/child care in arrears?			
How much are they currently legally obligated to pay in child support/child care?			
How do they distribute their net pay each pay day?			
What are their vocational and socioeconomic dreams?			
What are their goals for the next 5-10 years?			
What do they consider the difference between dreams and goals?			

13-15 MONTHS OF DATING	A: Degree of Observation 0=no knowledge 1=some degree of knowledge or this item is not applicable to this person	B: Degree of Knowledge 0=not at all or very slightly 1=a little knowledge 2=an average knowledge 3=complete knowledge or this item is not applicable	C=Degree of Acceptance 0=not acceptable 1=very unpleasant 2=does not bother you much 3=completely acceptable or not applicable
What treatment have they received at hospitals, medical clinics, substance abuse treatment programs, Narcotics Anonymous, Alcoholics Anonymous, or by psychiatrists, psychologists, psychiatric social workers or mental health professionals? When and why were they treated?			
Do they wear any prostheses or artificial devices?			
How much do they watch sports, soap operas and weekly programs on television?			
How often do they gamble, travel, sleep each day, play golf, go shopping, or visit friends and relatives?			

13-15 MONTHS OF DATING	A: Degree of Observation 0=no knowledge 1=some degree of knowledge or this item is not applicable to this person	B: Degree of Knowledge 0=not at all or very slightly 1=a little knowledge 2=an average knowledge 3=complete knowledge or this item is not applicable	C=Degree of Acceptance 0=not acceptable 1=very unpleasant 2=does not bother you much 3=completely acceptable or not applicable
What sexual fantasies do they have?			
If known, what do they believe would be their sexual/ lovemaking pattern/ program?			
If known, what specific sexual acts do they expect to practice in marriage?			
What are their views on birth control during the marriage?			
What is the least number of days per week they would expect to have sexual intercourse with their spouse?			
Sub-total for months 13-15 (24 items): A # _____ B # _____ C # _____			

16-18 Months of Dating	A: Degree of Observation 0=no knowledge 1=some degree of knowledge or this item is not applicable to this person	B: Degree of Knowledge 0=not at all or very slightly 1=a little knowledge 2=an average knowledge 3=complete knowledge or this item is not applicable	C=Degree of Acceptance 0=not acceptable 1=very unpleasant 2=does not bother you much 3=completely acceptable or not applicable
What is the person's financial status?			
What savings accounts, checking accounts, IRAs, CDs, stocks, bonds, mutual funds, pensions, and other investments do they have?			
How much do they have in each account?			
When can copies of individual credit rating record, (ie; TRW, Equifax, Dun & Bradstreet, etc.), high school and college transcripts, tax returns (for the past 3 years), judgments of divorce, paternity orders, bankruptcy orders, resumes, and bank/investment statements for the past 6 months be exchanged?			

16-18 MONTHS OF DATING	A: Degree of Observation 0=no knowledge 1=some degree of knowledge or this item is not applicable to this person	B: Degree of Knowledge 0=not at all or very slightly 1=a little knowledge 2=an average knowledge 3=complete knowledge or this item is not applicable	C=Degree of Acceptance 0=not acceptable 1=very unpleasant 2=does not bother you much 3=completely acceptable or not applicable
What is their long-term financial plan?			
How do they feel about the distribution of their wealth before and after their death?			
How would they want to prepare their Last Will and Testament to allow for yourself, step-children, biological children, minor/adult children, organizations, siblings, extended relatives, friends, parents, etc.?			
How do they feel about life support systems, transplants and surgery?			
What was the style of discipline used toward them when they were young?			

16-18 MONTHS OF DATING	A: Degree of Observation 0=**no knowledge** 1=**some degree of knowledge** or this item is **not applicable** to this person	B: Degree of Knowledge 0=**not at all** or very slightly 1=a **little** knowledge 2=an **average** knowledge 3=**complete** knowledge or this item is **not applicable**	C=Degree of Acceptance 0=**not acceptable** 1=**very unpleasant** 2=**does not bother you much** 3=**completely acceptable** or not applicable
Who disciplined them?			
How did the person feel about the way they were disciplined?			
What are their thoughts about how they would discipline their own children?			
What is their overall potential or ability to (1) help a child deal with new situations, (2) help a child calm down, (3) recognize a child's needs, (4) produce feelings of security for a spouse and children, and (5) help children cope with fears?			

16-18 MONTHS OF DATING	A: Degree of Observation 0=no knowledge 1=some degree of knowledge or this item is not applicable to this person	B: Degree of Knowledge 0=not at all or very slightly 1=a little knowledge 2=an average knowledge 3=complete knowledge or this item is not applicable	C=Degree of Acceptance 0=not acceptable 1=very unpleasant 2=does not bother you much 3=completely acceptable or not applicable
What is their overall potential or ability to (1) create feelings of confidence for those in the family home, (2) be a patient listener, (3) be a reliable source of love, and (4) aid and assist your family and their own family?			
Overall, how well would they consistently follow through with (1) enforcing homework assignments with children, and (2) setting bedtime limits?			

16-18 MONTHS OF DATING	A: Degree of Observation 0=no knowledge 1=some degree of knowledge or this item is not applicable to this person	B: Degree of Knowledge 0=not at all or very slightly 1=a little knowledge 2=an average knowledge 3=complete knowledge or this item is not applicable	C=Degree of Acceptance 0=not acceptable 1=very unpleasant 2=does not bother you much 3=completely acceptable or not applicable
Overall, how well would they consistently follow-up in areas such as (1) doing household chores, (2) paying household bills in a timely manner, (3) paying city, state and federal income taxes on time, (4) securing automobile license tabs on time, and (5) renewing their driver's license?			
Overall, what were the main problems in their home when they were age Birth-1 year, 1-3 years old, 4-5 years old, 6-11 years old, 12-20 years old, 20-24 years old, and 25-65 years old?			

16-18 MONTHS OF DATING	A: Degree of Observation 0=no knowledge 1=some degree of knowledge or this item is not applicable to this person	B: Degree of Knowledge 0=not at all or very slightly 1=a little knowledge 2=an average knowledge 3=complete knowledge or this item is not applicable	C=Degree of Acceptance 0=not acceptable 1=very unpleasant 2=does not bother you much 3=completely acceptable or not applicable
In their family home, who was generally responsible for cooking, cleaning, writing the checks to pay bills, disciplining the children? Do they believe the distribution of responsibilities was effective and right?			
Sub-total for months 16-18 (18 items): A # _____ B # _____ C # _____			

Sum Sub-totals Per Box Columns

Transfer of Sum Sub-totals:

A _____ + B _____ + C _____ =Score: _____

INTERPRETING YOUR FDAA SCORE

The ultimate actualization score is 1050 points. Because the Pre-Marital Screening Questionnaire (PSMQ) is a self-assessment test, the score is reliable only if there is honesty and a full, complete exchange of information between the dating parties. Low Full Disclosure and Acceptance (FDAA) scores are indicative of mere Pleasure Dating. High FDAA scores may indicate effective Investment Dating, or they could indicate a tendency to view the dating partner more favorably than is warranted—putting them in an unrealistically positive light. A high FDAA score, due to a pattern of excessive "not applicable" ratings, may reflect a failure to believe or accept the premise that full and honest discovery during courtship and dating can reduce the degree of marital discord, frustration, anger and bewilderment often experienced after marriage. High FDAA Scores also could be the product of giving the maximum rating (i.e., a 3) on items that are partially known instead of fully known.

INTERPRETATION GUIDELINES

EXPLANATION	SCORES
These are typical scores for those who are	**920 - 1050**
engaged in Investment and Biblical Dating, and it would appear that discussions about becoming engaged to enter into the covenant of marriage are appropriate after dating 12-18 months.	
These are typical scores for those who are	**790 - 919**
engaged in Investment Dating, but pre-marital or couple counseling is recommended to address individual differences before discussions about engagement or marriage should occur.	

These are typical scores for those who are   **660 - 789**

> engaged in mere Pleasure Dating. It would appear that gathering more information and knowledge of the person is needed before any discussions about engagement or marriage should occur.

These are very low scores and the parties are   **0 - 659**

> merely engaged in Pleasure Dating and appear to be avoiding all unpleasant discussions about their personal and family histories.

NOTES:

A person who is still looking good after the investigative dating period (typically, another three to six months) then becomes a candidate for "Investment Dating," the period in which two people begin to invest significant and exclusive time to determine whether they agree to put each other in the "Winner's Circle" of marriage.

Biblical Courtship: A Covenant and a Promise

Biblical courtship or marital commitment is the outgrowth of one's free will that is manifested in an informed, intellectual, emotional, and God-led decision to engage in a covenant promise and a trusting relationship with another. A biblical marital commitment or covenant has certain rights, privileges, duties and obligations, and is binding. The unfortunate reality, however, is that far too many married persons have tried to maintain a single life style. Many of them have been bound by a "fear-to-commit" stronghold.

Fears of Commitment

People are different and have individual needs. Therefore, their level of commitment to one another varies. Often males, and, to a lesser degree, females, cannot verbalize but will exhibit or act out reasons why it is difficult for them to make a commitment to marry and to remain married.

Single men and women alike are afraid to commit. Some fear is healthy and well-founded; however, irrational fears or fears based on misconceptions can hinder a person's ability to form lasting relationships. In our counseling work we have uncovered a number of fears and misconceptions about commitment. For each of these fears we provide words of guidance and suggested remedies to shatter each stronghold.

Misconceptions about the institution of marriage

Men and women have created the myth that the institution of marriage will be the cleansing power for all deficiencies and problems that they were subjected to in their single life. They make the mistake of believing that each day of marriage will be a good day and just loving each other will make everything right.

Remedy: God gave marriage as a gift which serves three purposes: (1) to leave your parents and unite together in a public ceremony; (2) to accept mutual responsibility for each other's welfare and to love the mate above all others; and (3) to unite into oneness in the intimacy and commitment of sexual union that is reserved for marriage (from the Life Application Study Bible, New Living Translation). Strong marriages include all three elements of unity. Marriage is a calling and not merely a desire of the heart.

Fearing the loss of control over life style, activities, money, body, freedom of movement, property, etc.

Remedy: This fear usually arises when an individual fails to focus on the fact that all that we have belongs to God, and we are merely the stewards of our earthly possessions. The remedy is to stop loving the world and all that it offers, for when we love the world, we show that we do not have the love of God—a spirit greater than ourselves. The world offers only physical pleasure and pride of possession. We should not lose focus on our status as stewards. Our material accomplishments are *not* the sole end-product of our creative hands.

Fear that marriage will become boring and that they will miss out on something in life.

Remedy: To maintain a healthy and rewarding relationship, an individual must learn how to be tolerant of the mediocre or boring times in a relationship or marriage and to aggressively plan to transform insecure and unexciting times into joy and happiness. You must avoid the haunts of those who would come between you and your partner, especially during boring times. Turn away and go somewhere else, for evil people cannot sleep until they have done their evil deed for the day. They cannot rest unless they have caused someone like you to stumble (see I Peter 5:8).

Fear of feeling trapped and losing a sense of self.

Remedy: When you focus on developing your relationship with God, you will gain a strong sense of self and the will that God has for your life. Seek people who have that focus; it will make for an equal "yoke" and enhance your individuality.

Becoming overly critical and "picky" when deciding on a mate.

Remedy: As a single person, pray for an answer and always know what God has confirmed as your "bottom line," your standard for a spouse. You know the person must love the Lord and your family. You know they must be born again. You know that finances are important. You know that there is a certain way you should be treated. Then, simply trust in the Lord with all of your heart and do not be impressed with your own wisdom (see Proverbs 3:5).

Intolerance of others.

Remedy: You may be so stressed in your personal or professional life that you cannot bear to even be around others. Be careful here; the tendency toward this trait increases with age. To overcome intolerance, you must experience a spiritual renewal of our thoughts and attitudes. Concentrate on being kind to each other, tenderhearted, compassionate, forgiving one another, just as God through Christ has forgiven us (as described in Colossians 3:12-14). Also, it can be helpful to do a "reality check:" How many people have to tolerate our own faults when they would much rather not? It's a hard question, but the answer may help you to be less persnickety.

Feeling overprotective of personal finances.

Remedy: The Word of God (Matthew 25:14-30) tells us that those who use well what they are given will be given even more, and they will have an abundance. It goes on to say that from those who are unfaithful, even what little they have will be taken away. The key to keep in mind is that personal finances should be disbursed responsibly, whether married or not. God blesses us with financial and non-financial resources so that we may invest them wisely toward the fulfillment of His purpose for our lives. God has equipped us to handle all the finances and resources He places in our care and stewardship. Overprotectiveness of personal resources is the bad fruit of our fears, feelings of insecurity, selfishness and self-centeredness. And if we are not righteously focused on the proper purpose and allocation of our monies, such thoughts and feelings will take our lifestyles—and our monies—out of the will of God.

Feeling too stressed-out to juggle one more thing.

Remedy: You will experience difficulty in handling the many balls you juggle in life each day without a sense of purpose, mission and peace. Peace of mind comes when we learn how not to worry about anything; but instead to pray about everything. Tell God what you need, and thank Him for all he has done (see Philippians 4:6-7). This requires consistent practice. And no, it is not easy.

Worrying that marriage will coerce personal change.

Remedy: You can't hurry love or build up to marriage too quickly. Love and marriage both require time. The proper perception is that marriage brings as a gift rewarding and positive change that allows partners to find favor with each other, as well as encourage, help, patronize, assist, uphold and foster each other. When two people come into a relationship, there is a tendency to want to make improvements or changes in each other. Early on in the relationship a decision needs to be made—preferably by both partners—that you can't change one another into people that you want each other to be. It is best to move in the direction of compromise and mutual acceptance. As the husband and wife submit to one another, they will become one spirit, one flame, and reflect each other as two lights that join together.

Clashing values and lifestyles.

Remedy: Adequate fellowship and dating time spent together will reveal if value and lifestyle differences are too significant to consider marriage as a feasible option. And remember, you should never want to be with anyone who doesn't want to be with you.

Feeling uncertain as to who is really going to be in control in the marriage.

Remedy: Those who seek a biblically-based marriage will rest assured in the Word of God that the husband is the head of his wife as Christ is the head of his Body, the Church. The husband must love his wife as he loves himself, and the wife must respect her husband and submit to her husband (see Ephesians 5:22-27). As the wife follows her husband, the husband shall follow Christ—He is the one who should really be in control of the marriage.

Lacking personal and professional success at this point in life.

Remedy: Remain mindful that all of us should grow to know the voice of God and meditate on His Word. The same God who takes care of us will supply all our needs from his glorious riches which have been given to us in Christ Jesus (Philippians 4:19). We should know what we want in life and what we need in order to achieve our personal and professional goals. Then, we should study, prepare and ask God for it.

Being afraid that the partner will not completely accept and support their personal goals and dreams.

Remedy: In marital counseling couples repeatedly remind us that they see themselves as competitors and not as partners. Instead of focusing on the acceptance of others, we should be loyal to Christ, honor Him and seek only His acceptance. We should then hold close to our breasts those that encourage, assist, and foster us in reaching our goals.

Recognizing the difficulty in finding a person who has a solid relationship with God.

Remedy: God's commandment to us is that we love one another as He has loved us (John 13:34). We need to understand that marriage is not just two bodies coming together, but the coming together of two spirits, two souls, and yes, two families. Love and marry your spirit complement—your soul mate. For the Christian, this is only possible with one who has a relationship with God through Jesus Christ. If your fear has to do with the fact that none of the people you encounter meet this basic requirement, your fear is healthy and well-founded.

Being unable to read people correctly and biblically.

Remedy: People often marry on the basis of "phileo" love that reacts to what is being done to them instead of "agape" love which is focused on the needs of the beloved. Study well who is meeting your spiritual, mental, emotional, intellectual, physical and material needs as a way to discriminate "phileo" lovers from "agape" lovers.

Fearing that a spouse will not be focused at home.

Remedy: Some people are unable to view the marital home as a place of refuge. Instead they see the home as a place to have physical needs met (e.g., food, shelter and sex) and personal property stored (e.g., clothing and other possessions). Such persons view their home as a "last resort" for recreation instead of the first and preferred point for their leisure activities. Study well who hastens to your side in comparison to who is with you only when it is convenient. This will tell you who views you as "home."

Lacking model marriages to emulate.

Remedy: Welcome an opportunity to change generational curses. An inability to form lasting marital partnerships is certainly one of the most devastating generational curses. It is essential for people who have not witnessed good marriages to find happy, spiritually focused couples and spend time with them.

Fearing a lack of honest disclosure by others, leading to a lack of trust.

Remedy: Study, understand and discuss with the person how others have broken the veil of trust with them since birth. And then love them enough to help them heal from those wounds. Be careful to keep your word so that they can trust you.

Having subconscious, fear-provoking dreams about marriage.

Remedy: By humbling yourself and freely submitting yourself to a higher authority, you will break this stronghold of fear.

Failing to recover from divorce or past failed relationships.

Divorce is one of the most traumatic experiences we can face—even the most scientific studies and accounts verify this. Victims of divorce or recurrent failed relationships often suffer from a sort of "Post Traumatic Relationship Disorder." Divorce is a severe emotional experience that can have lasting psychological effects long after the judge has finalized the decree. As with those who suffer from the clinical condition known as "Post Traumatic Stress Disorder," divorced people often feel that their personal survival, assets, or reputation are being threatened. Simply the word "marriage" may provoke physical reactions: irritability, angry outbursts, difficulty concentrating or an inability to sleep. It is difficult to socialize with and date such divorcees who often will ramble on about recurrent, distressing recollections of the last spouse or significant other. They are quick to describe the vivid images, thoughts and perceptions about their former date or spouse. And the flashback episodes usually will cause intense distress and emotional withdrawal. Because they feel it necessary to detach themselves emotionally, they cannot even consider talking about the "M" word. The tragic result? An inability to love.

Remedy: To banish and dislodge the stronghold of a fear to commit, you must first commit everything you do to the Lord. Trust Him, and He will help you (see Proverbs 16:3). For each of us to eradicate this stronghold, we must practice goodness, not speaking evil of others, but instead demonstrating love, humility, and submission. We must be wise and discerning of the other person's character and integrity. After making our decision, we should learn how to be humble and submit our lives to our God. The result: the ability to commit without fear.

If you do not overcome the above fears to commitment, and if you do not learn the answers to the items on the aforementioned PMSQ, then you willingly and intentionally assume the risk that those unknown areas may present a problem in your marriage. The best time to learn about the person in-depth and confront your own fears is *before* you get married. Take the blinders off your eyes; get beyond the good feelings that you have about the person. If you feel this person is your soul mate, then do not be afraid to ask them hard questions.

> **Marital Secret: If you marry prematurely, you will have to choose to accept what you did not try to learn about beforehand.**

Courtship must be a time of examination. An extended courtship allows you to view each other when either of you is sick, when one or the other is receiving public recognition, when one is experiencing a crisis, etc. You will find out how well the other person is able to control their appetites and desires as the relationship becomes more physically intimate. If they cannot control themselves before marriage, you know that it will be difficult for them after marriage. You may ask, "Why should we need to control our desires *after* marriage? After all, isn't it okay then?" Of course it is. But what if one of you gets sick? For an extended period? What about trips away from each other? What about pregnancy and newborns? If you do not think you will have to exhibit some amount of self-control after you get married, you are sorely mistaken and bound for a huge awakening, if not disappointment.

It is all right if you choose to face up to and accept the other person's deficiencies. But it is *not* all right to get married and then complain about what you don't like, what you didn't know, or what you don't understand about your spouse. When you have an intended spouse or Invested Dater who recognizes their major deficits and sincerely desires to eliminate them, then work with them *before* marriage. You will find out whether changes are long-lasting, acceptable and comfortable for you and the other person. The time frame for correcting the deficits should be determined by the person making the change in their life—not dictated by the other person. However, when you are not married, each party has a free-will choice to stay or to leave the relationship if the time frame for correction becomes cumbersome and too much to bear. And we need to be honest, consistent, straightforward and kind with the other person as to why we are terminating the relationship.

From a purely clinical standpoint, a score of 920 or higher on the PSMQ generally indicates that two people know enough about each other to get married. Also, to be considered is whether the two of you are at the point where each of you can communicate and elicit change in each other for the better. When you can make that kind of constructive interpersonal interchange and difference in another's life, it becomes a powerful indication and benchmark for making such a sacred and binding decision.

Chapter Two

Lies

In an effort to gain favor and impress a person romantically, often there are "half truths" or even blatant lies that are said in order to create a false or misleading impression. Many Pleasure Daters deliberately intend to deceive or confuse the issue. Such liars often make unreliable statements or insincere promises, or what they prefer to view as mere "white lies." But such spoken falsehoods damage and harm the relationship and ultimately the marriage.

In dating and in marriage, there must be consistent sincerity and truth in all actions, behaviors, emotions and thoughts.

Marital Secret: When you learn to let the truth run the show, you will be content and at peace regardless of the change in your marriage or in life circumstances around you.

The Wedding Altar Exercise: Unearthing the Golden Vessel of Problems

During our "Enhancing Romantic Relationships" workshops, we conduct a unique mock wedding vow exchange for the purpose of teaching what it means to "marry for better or for worse." The mock wedding ceremony teaches how two beautiful golden vessels or vases arranged before the minister can have a rich sheen and gold luster exterior even when filled with damaging traits and faults. When we see someone, we often remark about their outward handsomeness and beauty. However, we need to explore and know the inside of the person; we're not just marrying the rich sheen and golden luster.

A male and a female volunteer are solicited and a paper tuxedo and gown are draped and taped on the front of each volunteer. Each workshop participant is given an address label and asked to write one thing they do not like about their partner. The female workshop participants place their labels into one beautiful golden vessel or vase, and the male workshop participants place their labels into the other beautiful golden vessel or vase. After affixing each negative trait onto the paper attire for each gender, a mock wedding ceremony is performed. We have captured the results of several mock exercises below. In place of the negative behaviors included below, substitute things that bother you about your own partner. Pretend that at the altar you are making a vow to marry the person—your love interest—with all of their faults, both those you know for a fact, and those you would likely know about if you opened your eyes and inquired.

Standing at the wedding altar, the bride and groom appear as two beautiful golden vessels arranged before the minister and set in grand fashion before the assembly of relatives, associates and friends. We choose to use vessels because they make an elegant impression. Hand-formed with an artist's expertise and skill, they represent God's creation of human beings.

Vessels and vases often are covered with a final dark coating of glass after the piece has been annealed, etched and glazed.

Vases with subtle finishes or polished features vary from piece to piece. Frequently, vases are rich with natural colors to convey the qualities of strength and age. Whether coated with an artificial color or presented with rich natural colors, the character of each human vessel or vase is glazed by layers of life experiences. Our character is reflected by how we handle the fires and tribulations of life experiences.

Our vessels may flourish in beautiful colors on the surface, giving only the illusion that it they are made out of solid material. It is best when beautiful colors are both on the surface and beneath the surface. For when life applies fire, our durability and true substance are revealed, and our outer gold coating is unmasked either as metallic gold paint or the God-created resource of pure gold.

Here is a sample of one of our mock ceremonies:

I __, take you ___, to be my wedded wife (husband). To have and to hold, from this day forward, for better, for worse, for richer, for poorer, in sickness or in health, acknowledging before God and this assembly that I am aware of and totally dislike many of your ways such as your:

- Lying
- Not loving me for me
- Not supporting my personal growth and individuality
- Being guarded
- Not wanting to do anything
- Selfishness
- Lack of affection
- Not showing intimacy
- Low self-esteem resulting in extreme jealousy
- Being emotionally withdrawn
- Being easily discouraged when problems arise
- Teasing me about things that are serious to me
- Saying hurtful words and statements to me
- Inability to socialize
- Poor grammar

- Conservative politics
- Having too many questions
- Mismanaging money
- Not fully disclosing information
- Omission of the truth
- Lack of responsibility
- Being conflict-driven
- Avoiding what makes you upset
- Not talking about those things I do that upset you
- Negative attitude
- Inability to communicate and express your feelings
- Habit of breaking promises
- Not being educated enough
- Avoidance behavior
- Lack of goals
- Correcting my grammar
- Always being late and procrastinating
- Being inconsiderate of our time together
- Refusing to go places with me as a couple
- Comparing me to your ex-spouse and other men/women
- Being into yourself
- Being overly religious and talking about church and God all the time
- Greasing the pillow with your hair products
- Controlling behavior
- Defensiveness
- Possessiveness
- Being too short
- Being a substance abuser
- Refusing to make a full commitment
- Not attending church
- Different religious beliefs
- Being spoiled
- Being judgmental
- Being dishonest
- Not liking to have sex on a regular basis
- Not liking my friends

....but despite all of these things I do not like about you, I promise to love and to cherish you. I promise to be faithful to you, and to endeavor to show to you the same kind of love Christ showed the church when He died for her, and to love you as a part of myself because in His sight we shall be one. Despite all of the things I do not like about you today, I see you as my joy and my crown, and I give you all that I have—myself and my love— knowing that the previously mentioned faults may be problems in our marriage for the next 50-70 years, or 'till death do us part.

When you stand at the altar to marry a person, if you love that person just the way they are without them ever changing anything about them, then that truly is the person you should marry. If not, then you should not be marrying them. It is important to remain mindful that we marry the content and substance of the vessel or vase and not merely the beautiful and impressive outer appearance. At the altar we must sacrifice the selfishness of our individualism and sacrifice our single lifestyles. It is crucial that we accept and marry the other person's weaknesses and strengths, *without anticipation of change.*

Marital Secret: Marriage consists of mutual life long commitments and continuous personal sacrifices for the benefit of each other.

Lies We Tell Others:
The Different Faces of Infidelity

As children we become aware of our inner needs and expectations. However, when those inner needs are not satisfied by the realities of the environment, the "child self" is left with lifetime feelings of helplessness, confusion, instability, rejection, anxiety, frustration and lack of trust in others. That self ultimately will feel neglected and unloved. These disappointments and inconsistencies in a child's life may lead to feelings of emotional dependency, skepticism, and suspiciousness. The "adult self" may now be suffering the traumas of the "child self." And that is one reason why, as adults, we labor under marital problems.

As adults, our marriage expectations include positive attention, emotional expressiveness, respect, honor, regular physical intimacy, love and a fellowship type of companionship with our spouse. The person who gives these is the person we most want to be physically intimate with. Unfortunately, if our spouse fails to meet these needs, many of us will seek and find satisfaction elsewhere.

Infidelity can be viewed as a:

- Lack of loyalty to your partner,
- Marital unfaithfulness, and/or
- Transition from a partner-focused marriage to a (fill in the blank)- focused marriage.

It is important to face the reality that sexual dissatisfaction is most likely not the **only** cause for infidelity in the marriage. When there is not an unswerving allegiance to the marital vows and to the spouse, there may be any number of other causes, ranging from emotional distance to repeated arguments to outside pressures not necessarily related to the marriage. Also, many clients have shared with us that when any activity causes their spouse to be apart and distant from them, they fear infidelity. They assert that the feelings that are invoked are similar—if not identical—to those that arise in a spouse when their partner has been sexually intimate or unfaithful with someone other than themselves. Feelings experienced by the victim of infidelity may include:

- Loss
- Sadness
- Panic
- Dismay
- Rage
- Disappointment
- Guilt
- Bitterness
- Rejection

- Jealousy
- Emptiness
- Hurt
- Distrust
- Despair
- Helplessness
- Resentment
- Inadequacy
- Betrayal
- Fear
- Loneliness
- Abandonment

To those who have experienced the pain of infidelity, please listen to this: *Those same feelings of betrayal can occur even in circumstances where sexual infidelity is not the problem, but instead the spouse neglects their partner's emotional needs because of other interests, the children, work (paid and volunteer), church involvement, or extended family matters.*

It is important that marital partners fellowship with each other as much as possible, look inward to the marriage and minimize the demands that cause partners to socialize separately and be out of unity and fellowship with each other. There will be a stronger marriage when each spouse is intimately aware of all details, circumstances, pressures, thoughts and feelings of their respective partner. Know what's happening in your spouse's life; get daily updates. A strong marriage is realized when there is an integration of both individual lives by sharing and enjoying mutual interests, activities and life styles. There will be a strong marriage if there is joint time shared in unity with each other's families, friends and associates.

> **Marital Secret: The more time that a couple spends apart from each other, the greater the probability of marital discord, separation and/ or divorce.**

Lies We Tell Ourselves: Fantasies and Faulty Thoughts

Most people like harmony in their lives. We tend to like to be with people that think, feel and act like us because we make the mistake of believing that such similarity or homogeneity will validate our existence and our own character. However, each of us was born in completely different households, families or parts of the world. Each of us has unique thought patterns, emotional states and communication styles. Despite our obvious differences, we hold on to the fantasy that only people who think, feel and act like ourselves will be compatible with us.

One of our marital problems is that we think we can change a person to be more like us or our image of a proper spouse if we just give them enough love and nourishment. But this is not true. It is important to face the reality that your personal temperament and personality will probably not change after you marry. This is true even if the partners are equally yoked and compatible.

It is not fair to expect your spouse to meet your every need. It's not fair to your partner to place pressure on them to be your *everything*.

There are strongholds of fantasies and faulty thoughts that cause husbands and wives not to communicate well, and not to feel good about themselves and each other. It keeps us in bondage, wandering in a fog. Here are just a few:

- I must be perfect (but I am failing to recognize that only God is perfect for we have all sinned and come short of the glory of God, as Romans 3:23 reminds us).

- I must have everyone's love and approval (but seeking people's approval will cause me to change into someone I don't even recognize).

- My total personal worth equals the quality of each of my single performances in life (so any one failure on any one day would cause me to change and lower my self-esteem and self-image).

- Others are responsible for my personal problems and the negative consequences of my own behaviors and actions.

When divorce happens, the fantasies continue—except that they are about the ex-spouse:

- A belief that the divorced relationship can be re-established. (NOTE: This is not to say that no broken marriage can be made whole, only that it takes two people to do so.)

- A belief that making uncompromising demands on issues such as alimony, child support, child care, and economic issues will make the individual "feel" better and carry no consequences for the children.

- A belief that it will be easy to settle matters such as Last Wills and Testaments/Trusts in blended families.

- A belief that it is possible for second marriage couples to live in a house that was decorated by a former marriage partner.

- A belief that the next commitment/relationship/marriage must be perfect.

- A belief that inappropriate emotional/physical ties with the ex-spouse will bring peace and an end to loneliness.

When we allow ourselves to believe these lies, when we continue to allow external sources to miseducate us about ourselves, we won't be able to enjoy life richly. And when we lose our zest for life and our contentment in marriage then our marital relationships will continue to be impaired.

When Givers Marry Sole-Soul Takers

Marriage is a matter of give and take. But in the case of the "Sole-Soul Taker," we find a one-sided phenomenon. While one partner suffers, the Sole-Soul Taker avoids personal sacrifice. The Sole-Soul Taker dominates the relationship and never considers an equal partnership. Let us look at the behavior of Givers and Takers, as it relates to marital abuse, personal suffering and sacrifices.

Abuse is the mistreatment of one person by another or mistreatment of the self by deliberately seeking harmful conditions or substances. Far too often when we think about spousal abuse, we narrowly think about physical abuse. However, we must understand the full array of abusive acts in order to remain sensitive to the damage that results from mistreatment by others and ourselves. We need to remain sensitive to the fact that we can be abused physically, sexually, mentally, verbally or emotionally. We also can be abused by neglect.

The abuser often will be experiencing frustration, depression, loss of self-esteem, annoyance, threatening behavior or tension. The target of the abuse will often experience behaviors and feelings such as frustration, dependence, thoughts of suicide, depression, feelings of worthlessness, poor attention span, shame and hopelessness. Often both will feel in common depression, frustration, loss of self-esteem and loss of self-control.

Givers who marry selfish and abusive persons may also be abusing themselves. Some of the signs:

- Physical self-mutilation (placing self in harm's way).

- Alcohol abuse, illegal drug use (including steroids, cocaine, hallucinogens, cannabis, amphetamines, caffeine, inhalants, nicotine, heroin, phencyclicline and sedatives) and prescription drugs in order to cope with the abuse and stress in the marriage.

- Food—excessive eating or deprivation.

- Gambling—including lotteries, stock market "hot tips," and betting on sporting events.

- Spending money—cash, credit cards, checking accounts, "ATM" cards.

- Getting involved in unhealthy relationships.

- Sexual behavior—deviant, irresponsible, or excessive sex.

- Work—including excessive housework and excessive overtime.

When the Sole-Soul Taker is the dominating and authoritarian partner in the marriage, then they may cause the Giver to suffer. Interestingly, when the Giver is the dominating and authoritarian partner, then they may force the Sole-Soul Taker to make personal sacrifices.

There is a difference between suffering and personal sacrifice. The former is to be avoided; the latter, wisely and freely chosen. Suffering is unavoidable distress or pain, being forced to endure and sustain a personal loss or damage of something tangible or intangible. The time frame: no end in sight. And the loss just may be the soul and spirit of the Giver.

However, making a personal sacrifice is surrendering something for the sake of something or someone else. A personal sacrifice is something that one gives up—a free-will choice for a greater purpose or cause. And the sacrifice is only for a given time period. Givers frequently have a hard time telling the difference.

We often conduct surveys to find what our clients desire in a spouse. A female "Sole-Soul Taker" wrote down this list:

1. Loves me as funky as I am.

2. Will make me want to be the wife he needs.

3. Is a good provider and works hard.

4. Is educated with at least one degree, but preferably a master's degree.

5. Laid-back and easy to be with.

6. Has wisdom, power and good decision-making skills.

7. Doesn't complain to or about me.

8. Supportive of me unconditionally.

9. Has a good understanding of me and accepts me just as I am.

10. Handsome.

Unfortunately, the very qualities Sole-Soul Takers are looking for in a spouse are qualities that are missing in themselves. When asked, this same person saw herself as selfish, aloof, irritable, desirous of personal privacy and unwilling to sacrifice!

> **Marital Secret: We should be careful about what we expect in a relationship. We should not expect more in a spouse than we ourselves can provide.**

Givers should recognize that their Sole-Soul Taker spouse is addicted to receiving instead of giving. They need to recognize that their souls are being harmed by their relationship with the Taker. The Giver should face the co-dependent nature of the relationship, and resolve to take care of their own needs. They must seek their power from God who will provide and grant the inner strength needed. Above all, the Giver should renew their mind and hold the Sole-Soul Taker responsible for the consequences of the verbal and non-verbal behaviors that impact the marriage, and at the same time recognize and accept their partner's limitations and shortcomings.

That is a tall order. It takes courage, character and the wisdom that comes from God to walk the fine line between setting expectations and boundaries in a marriage and living peacefully with another's limitations. It is important that each partner in a marriage spontaneously gives and takes from each other so that the needs of each partner are recognized and met.

The Last Straw

"The covenant of marriage is breached when there has been a breakdown of the marriage relationship to the extent that the objects of matrimony have been destroyed and there remains no reasonable likelihood that the bonds of marriage can be preserved." This is the statutory language used in most divorce judgments. Divorce is damaging and often devastating—not only to the parties in the marriage but also to families, children, friends, church associates, co-workers and communities. Divorce is the silent parent to many social ills: abuse, shorter life spans, increase in the poverty rate, juvenile delinquency, mental illness and a host of other medical problems. All too often, it creates families that are dysfunctional.

Despite the risks, however, marriage continues to be a personal desire for 96 percent of the American population. However, it is reported that 65 percent of new marriages fail according to Maggie Gallagher, author of *The Abolition of Marriage*. She further informs us that the marriage rate has fallen nearly 30 percent since 1970 and the divorce rate has increased about 40 percent. This is despite the fact that fully 81 percent of divorced and separate persons believe that marriage should be for life.

This information draws a discouraging picture. Although nearly everyone would like to get married, more people are unwilling to take the risk of actually getting married. And for persons that assume the risk, 65 percent of those new marriages fail. According to the National Center for Health Statistics, as reported in September 2000, the United States divorce rate is 0.41 percent per capita per year and 10 percent of adult Americans are currently divorced.

The Barna Research Group has compiled massive research on families. They report statistics and analysis about divorce and Christians that dispel some myths about religion and divorce; specifically:

General Information Among the Churched and Unchurched Population:

☞ 54% of American adults are married.

☞ 11% of the adult population is currently divorced and has not remarried.

☞ 25% of all adults have experienced at least one divorce during their lifetime.

☞ 24% of adults have never been divorced (this includes persons who have never married, persons who have re mained married, widows and widowers).

☞ The divorce rate among both Christians and non-Christians has remained stable across the past half decade ending in 1999.

Christians Who Divorce:

☞ 27% of born again Christians, at the time of this writing, are or have previously been divorced.

☞ 26% of born again Christians have gone through a divorce some time in their lives.

☞ 65% of persons absolutely committed to the Christian faith are married.

☞ 64% of church attendees are married.

☞ 60% of born again Christians are married.

☞ The divorce rate among people who attend mainline Protestant churches is statistically no different than the national average of 25%.

Non-Christians Who Divorce:

☞ 24% of non-born again Christian adults, at the time of this writing, are or have previously been divorced.

👆 22% of non-Christians have gone through a divorce some time in their lives.

Stanley Rosenblatt, Esq., author of *The Divorce Racket*, a book published in 1969 advocating radical legal reforms in divorce, lists the seven most common grounds of divorce:

1. Cruelty

2. Desertion

3. Adultery

4. Alcoholism

5. Felony conviction

6. Nonsupport

7. Impotence

Divorce is a sad fact of life. To prevent its continued prevalence, it makes sense to study closely the factors that lead to divorce. Perhaps we will be able to see typical patterns and help others to avoid them. Generally we ask persons seeking legal counsel to pursue divorce to complete the "Finner-Williams Divorce Intent Survey" and allow the results to be released anonymously:

"Please write down the reason your marriage went wrong and what is now leading to a divorce. This information is confidential and you do not need to provide your name if you do not wish to be identified….The information we are gathering will help those who are attempting to save their marriages or who are seeking marital counseling."

A sample of typical responses by plaintiff divorcees follows. The risk factors for divorce are revealed in each of the following heart-filled testimonies:

• Our marriage went wrong because we grew apart after several attempts (three) to seek help. We did not change our lives to make our marriage a priority. He did not support my emotional needs, and I did not support his physical (sexual) needs.

- I believe that the true sanctity and meaning of the marriage vows were not enforced in her life. I also believe that our marriage was based on money and physical attraction, rather than spiritual content. It revolved around the wants and influence of her mother rather than our joint united bond to overcome any obstacles. She also carried some of her previous marriage baggage into our marriage. She has been holding my baby boy hostage to punish me for the problems between us that we could not work out while separated.

- This has been going on for years. I was beaten, controlled and dominated, yet I always believed he loved me, as I thought I loved him. He is the main reason my family went to prison, because we sold drugs. We should have quit, but we did not. He is not the total blame, but if he would have quit when I told him, we would not have lost everything we had. We would not have gone to prison. And, the family would not be torn apart. Since I have been free of him, I want to stay free. A burden was lifted off my heart, and I am happy to be free of him. I should not have waited until he went to prison, but I did not know what freedom was until we were separated. It should have happened 25 years ago. It took me too long to wake up. I could have been dead, because of fear. Don't let the same thing happen to you. Don't wait 30 years to see the light.

- He decided that he wanted to start seeing other women. The women started to harass me on the telephone as well as by mail. He wanted someone younger than myself. Because of the mental abuse from him, my life was turned upside down. Later in the marriage I found that he really didn't want anything out of life.

- I got a letter from him telling me about his past (that he is gay). Yes, I do know a lot about him but not about what is in this letter. He should have told me before we ever kissed, had a child, or even got married. He withholds information from me, and I don't feel it is right. I could no longer care for him the way I did. I could never love him or trust him again. And, to me, holding this from me is like playing a mind game. In his letter he states that he is gay and that he would understand if I no longer want him. It now makes me feel sick.

- I was paying all the bills and was tired of arguing every day.

- I came to my senses and realized that all of the effort that I had spent trying to reconcile differences and witnessing the unwillingness of my wife to compromise or change would have been an endless, torturous, painful process. So I got out of there. Who wants to be in pain forever when one party is not willing to compromise? Somebody had to be healthy.

- The love had died. There was no respect or trust in the marriage. There was a breakdown of everything my wife and I had built. There was a blatant disrespect for me, and my wife stopped the romance and lovemaking three years ago. That's kind of important to me.

- I filed for divorce because my wife threatened to keep my baby girl from me. We would go to church, and she claimed to be a Christian, but she has been manipulative by controlling my time with our daughter and with sex. She was self-serving for the entire marriage.

- My husband was cheating, was never home, was not a father, had other children before and after marriage, didn't take care of his family, just never was there when needed him. I could go on forever and ever.

- Our marriage went wrong because we had issues dealing with communication before we got married. This is something that should have been dealt with beforehand. Throughout this short marriage he has not found that marriage takes two people to work together. The togetherness was not there. There was no help with the bills, although he was working. He did not want me to go places or be around people that I normally would have been around. There was use of abusive words or actions. Also, when left to care for the kids, he always thought and said he was "babysitting." He was never willing to talk if I had an issue that I wanted to discuss with him; I had to wait until he was ready.

- There was lack of communication, loss of time spent together and affection, loss of trust, loss of respect, loss of honor. Needs were not being met. He stopped coming home. He ran up bills then paid slowly or neglected to pay. He believed he should pay himself first instead of bills. I believe bills should come first, then needs, then wants. There were long periods throughout the marriage with no sex. He stopped buying food. Our boys slept on a couch and loveseat instead of beds. I didn't feel loved, honored, desired or wanted.

- There was an obvious breakdown in the marriage. Some factors were a lack of communication/lack of willingness to compromise, squandering money, drug abuse and not building for the future. He was very controlling because I let him be. When times got rough, he wanted to bail out instead of what our marriage vows stated (for better or worse).

We must try to have a zest for life and marriage by controlling, handling and tolerating the different circumstances that arise in marriage. We must train our minds not to wander and imagine things that have not really happened. We must make sure our relationships with God and others are in order. We must not let life's demands overwhelm us.

The Word of God, in Philippians 4:8 (KJV) tells us that we should think only on things that are true, honest, just, pure, lovely, or of good report, virtuous, and praiseworthy. We should practice limiting our thoughts to these eight things. We choose our emotions, and no one can make or provoke us to think, feel or react contrary to the Word of God without our conscious decision to give up personal power and self-control. We must be disciplined in our thought life in order to have a healthy and happy marriage.

Chapter Three

Communication

Our words, tone of voice, behavior, and physical and facial expressions all transmit messages. Communication can be expressed intentionally or accidentally. Intentional communication occurs when a person deliberately sets out to convey a specific meaning or impression. Accidental communication occurs when a person conveys a specific meaning or impression without intending to do so. In marriage we need to watch our words, tone of voice and delivery style so that communication will not shut down between the partners.

Our mother, Trudie Sue Williams, gives some wise, humorous advice: "When you have a spouse who deliberately fails to communicate with you or is negative for a long period of time, one day just take all your clothes off and continue doing your regular activities. Wash dishes, fold clothes, cook, pay bills, dust—but do it butt naked." She promises that laughter will inevitably follow, and communication will not be far behind. She personally practiced this technique for 57 years of marriage. As clinicians we have shared the same advice and are pleased with the numerous successful testimonies that have come forth. We encourage you to attempt this tested and proven communication enhancement technique!

Communication, Criticism and Confrontation Styles

There are two different ways to communicate with your spouse: verbally and non-verbally. Our verbal communication styles are determined by our tone of voice and our pattern or rate of speech. Our non-verbal communication styles are determined by body language, posture, the physical space that exists between the speaker and receiver, timing and environmental setting. It is important that we manage ourselves verbally and non-verbally. We must learn how to confront and criticize the wrong behavior or issue and not the partner that we love. Allow yourself to be molded by the Holy Spirit so that your tongue can be bridled, instead of being sharp or acidic.

It is our belief that if we foster our first seven words with love and edification, we will reduce the probability of a criticism or negative confrontation. There are several examples of wicked, vicious or ungodly manners of speech that will damage and destroy a marriage. Examine yourself to make sure you are not employing the following:

- Exhibiting puffed-up conduct; such as thinking of yourself more highly than you should.

- Having a prideful and arrogant attitude that causes you to believe that your point of view is the only correct position and causes you to be insensitive to your spouse.

- Judging and blaming your partner for specific actions before correcting your own behaviors and actions that damage the marriage.

- Lying to yourself and your spouse in an effort to justify your wrong actions, emotions and thoughts.

- Knowingly and intentionally lying when you believe that the truth will not be sufficient and persuasive enough.

- Being impulsive, easily provoked, too quick to anger and too quick to accuse your spouse.

- Displaying bitterness, strife (i.e., suffocating discouragement and a strong competitive force against your spouse) and wrath (i.e., strong, vengeful anger or indignation, self-imposed punishment against your spouse for their offensive behavior).

- Performing foolish and senseless destructive acts with reckless disregard for the consequences of your conduct on your marriage.

> **Marital Secret: We can choose our behaviors, but we cannot choose the consequences of our behaviors.**

Criticism and confrontation are usually communicated with words, and words can hurt. Learn how to shorten your arguments, especially those that repeat themselves. Learn how to discuss your differences with the same "natural interactive" speech style and speech pattern that you use when you're happy, communing with each other in love. That will be a challenge. If you don't argue in a natural interactive mode, then usually you will resort to a "lecture format" style of arguing. That's when one spouse is speaking and the other spouse is listening but gearing up for a rebuttal. This style of arguing is merely venting and a waste of time if you want to achieve closure.

Name calling is often a last resort. We suggest that you call your spouse by their surname (Mrs. Jones or Mr. Jones) instead of the derogatory name. The tone of voice may start off a little rough, but with practice you will learn in time how to deliver it with sweetness and then with compassion. In the midst of our pain and being critical, we need to protect and encourage each other with positive words, not degrading each other with defamatory labels that leave our spouses feeling dehumanized.

Our aunt, Bernice Finner McAdoo, has a ministry of writing and communicating to newlyweds a specific word of advice:

"Don't be a switchblade or razor blade mama or papa.

You can cut a person with your tongue, and their emotional wound needs to heal first before your tongue speaks to them again. Don't talk to your spouse while they're wounded, hurting and angry. Say 'I'm sorry' and then wait in loving silence until your spouse's feelings have settled. Wait to restart your discussion of the problem until there has been enough time for your spouse to separate their thoughts and opinions from the emotional pain, hurt and harm that they felt earlier. Don't engage your spouse in conflict resolution sooner than when they are ready to do so. It may take one to three days—or it may take a week. Just like a deep finger cut, emotional cuts also need an antiseptic, an antibiotic, a bandage and time to heal. Emotional cuts need protection from further harmful conditions or weakness. Emotional cuts need enriching qualities, the cover of Jesus and patience by the spouse."

These are the words of a mature and wise counselor.

Chiseling Away at the Spirit

Let's go back to some of the words we heard people say to each other earlier in this book: "Why did I marry you?" "How could you be so stupid?" When these kinds of words are spoken too often, the result is a chiseling away at the spirit of a person. The critical spouse may be paranoid, defensive or angry. They believe that they are right and they expect their spouse to behave as they expect them to. They believe that everything is fine with them and that their spouse has a problem. Such critical and unfair spouses cause their partners to feel frustrated, threatened and uncertain about their self-worth.

To such critical persons we say this: When you verbally degrade and put down your spouse, you also discredit yourself. You chose to marry the person; what does that say about your judgment and decision-making skills?

Communication styles and marital concerns between a couple must be given equal attention to resolve them successfully and completely. The way we speak is dependent on how we are conditioned in life. Your spouse may hear your statement but distort its meaning based on their personal history and orientation. You must press yourself to love your mate regardless of personal issues, problems, concerns, challenges and situations that occur in their lives. And resolution of conflicts must be done in a manner that does not demolish your mate's self-esteem or chisel away at their spirit.

Despite our individual differences, for the sake of the marriage we must learn how to fight and argue in healthy ways. Let us offer some constructive ways to talk without fighting and resolve marital conflicts:

1. Remain mindful that husbands and wives cannot be silent and work out their marital problems at the same time. But also remember not to exaggerate the problem when you discuss it with your spouse.

2. Manage the intensity and tone of your voice so that they are no greater than the "smoothing" flow of brook water. A gentle voice will chase away stress and create tranquil marital sounds in the home. Irritating voice tones will build walls between spouses. Spouses often hold to the myth that elevation and intensity of their voice will give more validity to their opinion. Choose to speak with your best romantic (not sexy) voice. Stay calm, kind and peaceful.

3. Regardless of your spouse's personal choices and conduct, you must maintain a personal desire to change yourself. You must desire to change your own thoughts, emotions and behaviors. You personally must believe that through your Lord and Savior Jesus Christ you have sufficient personal power to become a new creature in Christ—a new spouse despite the negative atmosphere around you. Your personal change can be immediate—yes, as quick as tomorrow morning—when you rise and are given new mercies. Philippians 4:13 encourages us with

these words; "For I can do everything with the help of Christ who gives me the strength I need" (NLT).You must practice this new attitude daily, consistently, intensely and faithfully. I Chronicles 28:10 (NLT) tells us to "consider now, for the Lord has chosen you to build a temple as a sanctuary. Be strong and do the work." In other words, just change. Just behave as God directs us to behave. To use a trademark phrase, "Just do it." And keep doing it until you have changed.

4. Talk directly with your spouse about the problem. Attack the problem and not the person associated with the behavior or problem. Avoid using the word "you" when expressing your feelings about an issue.

5. Be careful not to drone on and on. People tend to lose interest after the first 30 seconds of speech.

6. Be humble—you just may be wrong. It is important to repent and say you are sorry when you are wrong. Learn how to discern and banish the demons that influence you. All of us have sinned and come short of the glory of God (Romans 3:23). Demonic and evil spirits cannot share space with the Holy Spirit.

7. You must stay focused on what is good in your marriage while you are resolving marital problems. This will give you hope.

8. Be specific about the problem. Stay focused on the subject or issue at hand and don't stray or regress to other issues from the past. Make your point once and don't belabor your opinion on the issue. Be mindful that several things or stressors in your spouse's life are competing for their attention, even as you speak.

9. It is important to have a clean heart which indicates your true motivation. Similarly, you should learn to consider the heart of your spouse instead of negatively reacting to and being blinded by your spouse's destructive and demonic behavior. What your heart thinks on is what will come out of your mouth. If you communicate destruction, your heart will expect the

downfall of the relationship. You must change your heart, your motivation—and your hope.

10. Reduce the number of negative people and negative influences that are in your lives. What you read, watch, listen to, and how you live will influence your ability to communicate with others and resolve marital problems.

11. Develop your own marital style for conflict resolution. For some, sarcasm will work effectively. For others, it may be humor. Still others take an intellectual approach, a dramatic approach, or a rational emotional reflection. Your argument or discussion style should not be compared to the style of family members and friends.

12. Understand that the power of life and death are in the tongue. You can speak life to your situation or your spouse and make things better or worse for both you and your spouse—or at least for you.

13. Establish non-negotiable communication guidelines, promises and boundaries. Agree that no form of abuse is acceptable from either spouse. Be faithful to your intra-marital or interpersonal covenants and hold each party to the promises made.

14. Always offer a solution along with your constructive criticism.

15. Show interest in each other, edify each other and tell your partner what you appreciate about them numerous times during the day.

16. Take a physical time out within the home if the discussion cannot be handled by both parties at the time or if the verbal disagreement becomes too intense and emotional.

17. Count to ten in silence before you respond to your partner's speech. When you speak, only speak the truth in the spirit of love and gentleness. When verbally and wrongfully criticized, try to respond with questions instead of responding with de-

fensive comments or statements. If the criticism is correct, then respond with agreement.

18. Respect your spouse's right to have an opinion that may differ from yours. You were raised in two different houses by two different families, and you have two different personal histories, which have made a direct impact on the formulation of your values, morals, thoughts and feelings. There must be an honest recognition, acknowledgment, acceptance and mutually agreed-upon approach by the couple in order to cope with and handle incompatibilities, disagreements and differences. It is important to realize that such incompatibilities will probably not change much during the course of the marriage.

Don't lose hope or faith if your marital problems cause you to be frustrated, angry, hostile or drained in your spirit. If your behavior doesn't resemble that of Jesus, repent, ask for forgiveness from your spouse and God, and live a higher life again. Feelings shift from anger to fear to triumph. Words can affect your spirit, self-esteem and soul. Therefore, confess your sins—your ungodly speech—to each other and pray for each other so that you and your marriage may be healed. The prayers of a righteous man and woman are powerful and effective (see James 5:16 KJV).

Marital Soul-Esteem

Just as you can have self-esteem, you can also have marital "soul-esteem"—the direct result of the regard we hold for our marital partner and our marriage. Marital soul-esteem has to do with how we perceive ourselves in the marriage and how we feel about the marriage. There can be positive or negative marital soul-esteem, depending on if there is a high opinion or low value placed on the spiritual principles and essence of the marriage. The charts below illustrate the differences:

Persons with high marital soul-esteem...

• feel that they have a great influence on the judgments and opinions of their spouse.

- feel that they can achieve goals and objectives within the boundaries of the marriage.

- feel like an efficient, equal and competent partner in the marriage.

- feel as if they are held in high regard and have the favor of God and of their marital partner.

- feel that they are praised by their partner for their total spirit, self, emotional responses, judgment, thoughts, opinions and passion.

Low marital soul-esteem will cause a partner to...

- feel annoyed, powerless, dehumanized and alienated in the marriage.

- feel like a competitor with their spouse.

- feel incompetent and like a victim of constant verbal criticism.

- feel inferior and intimidated by their partner.

- feel neglected, forgotten and overlooked by their partner within and outside of the marital home.

Money and education are two factors that make a difference in how partners regard their marriages. Differences in the way two people were raised, not only economically but culturally, can lead to differences in each partner's marital soul-esteem levels. If one or the other makes significantly less money or has significantly less formal education, the couple often finds reasons for conflict beyond the norm—especially if the higher earning or higher-educated spouse looks down on or does not honor the other.

But economics and culture are not the only reasons that couples may not have a stellar opinion of their marriage. Here are some other "marriage-defeating" factors:

- Lack of empathy or appreciation.

- Controlling or oppressive behavior by one or both partners.

- Different work tolerance and sleeping needs.

How can you improve your martial soul-esteem levels? Here are some daily "marital vitamins" you can take:

Marital Secret: The Key "Vitamins" for Marital Health:

Vitamin A: **A**ccept constructive criticism and changes within the marriage. **A**lways be willing to forgive, reconcile, and then perfect yourself within the institution of marriage so that your new and improved self can be used in service to God. **Vitamin C:** **C**ultivate the ability to self-counsel and encourage. **Vitamin K:** **K**now what it means for God to love you. **Vitamin L:** **L**augh and share humor with each other daily. **Vitamin M:** **M**aintain a clean heart, clean hands, reasonable emotions and pure thoughts. **M**ake sure you do something to edify, aid, or promote your spouse.	**Vitamin R:** **R**elax, recreate, and get sufficient sleep and proper nourishment. (This is more important than you think!) **R**emain flexible. **Vitamin S:** **S**pend quality time together. In our society we invest excessive monies to secure our automobiles and homes with padlocks, iron rods at windows, iron security guards on doors, loud alarm systems, guard dogs and other protective devices. However, it is interesting to note that we do not provide comfortable security and safeguards for our marriages. We can safeguard our marital soul-esteem by maintaining a marital environment that will assure that each partner has a high regard for the marriage and feels a sense of worth and value from the other.

Twelve Ways Men and Women are Different

Cynthia Taueg, RN, BSN, MPH, of the "Glory To God Ministries" is author of *Planting Seeds for the Harvest of a Successful Marriage: A Guide for Women.* She has outlined what she perceives as the general differences between men and women:

MEN AND WOMEN ARE DIFFERENT	
WOMEN	**MEN**
Role Is Helper	Role Is Provider, Protector
First Priority Is Relationship	First Priority Is Competition
Personal	Apart/More Alone
Greater Vitality	50% Stronger/More Muscle
Sexually Stimulated by Touch and Words	Sexually Stimulated Visually
Intuitive, Perceptive of Details	Logical, Big Picture Focus
Communicates through Words	Communicates through Actions
Socially Aware	Task-Centered
Problem-Oriented (Wants to Know Why)	Solution-Oriented (Fix It Quickly)
Wants to Be Right— Focus on How It Should Be	Wants to Do What Works— Practical
Responds to Romance	Responds to Admiration
Complex, Intricate	Simple, Basic

Taueg shares with women many tried-and-true principles of successful relationships when she writes:

"We sow seeds of love for our husbands by finding and fulfilling his distinctive needs. Each man is unique so the specifics must come from him. However, the

categories of need are basically the same:
1. To be loved, emotionally and sexually
2. To be admired
3. To be accepted as he is
4. To feel appreciated

"When these needs are met, he feels good about himself. He has a sense of well-being. He will then be more likely and able to meet your needs. He will not want to do his job unless he is 'paid.' This pay involves the four points mentioned above, which include sex as just one component. You make being in a relationship with you rewarding when you boost his ego. When his needs are not met, he will demonstrate fight or flight behavior. If you complain, nag or try to control him and get him to do everything on your terms, he may resist you actively or passively because his ego is threatened. When his needs are met without complaint, he will usually compromise or give you what you want. Remember that his needs usually must be met first. When this is done consistently and lovingly, he will do more and more to please you to get his reward; namely, admiration, appreciation, acceptance and affection. Where there are no rewards, he will be a reluctant giver...

"'What about me and my needs?' you say. 'I give and give and give' or 'I tried and have gotten bad or no results.' Remember to take a look at how you tried before. Most likely it was not from the point of view of meeting his needs in a way it could be received. Also, remember this is not a 50/50 proposition. We must give 100 percent. What's written herein is based on God's Word and has been tried and tested as to its bringing beneficial results in marriage. It's a very different point of view and approach than what the world believes. We must try again and do it God's way."

Men and women, for the most part, don't understand their gender or individual differences. A husband who honors his wife will protect, respect, help and stay with his wife and be sensitive to her needs. He will relate to her with courtesy, consideration, insight and tact. If a man does not treat his wife kindly, his prayers become ineffective, because everything relates to one's relationship to God (I Peter 3:7-12 KJV). When a spouse's priority relationship is to God and that relationship is right with God, then their relationship will be right with others, including the most important human relationship: their spouse.

In I Peter 3:7 (NLT), when Peter referred to the wife as the weaker sex, he did not mean that she is inferior. He was merely acknowledging the wife's greater vitality, her physical limitations and her vulnerability to various kinds of assaults and abuses. These can range from sexual abuse to discriminatory harassment in the workplace.

Men, choose your words carefully and touch your wives romantically without any sexual overtones. Understand that getting "on top of" your spouse physically is not getting on top of the marriage. Husbands must communicate with wives through words and touch in order to work through the marital problems. Women want to be in tune spiritually with the man before becoming physical or sexual. Making love to your mate physically doesn't entirely resolve the problems resulting from other major areas of concern.

And, to the wives: A good wife responds and adapts to her husband. She cares for his needs and prays for him diligently. She keeps a peaceful home and sees herself as his partner in life. She looks for ways to help him achieve his goals. She sees to it that the needs of the home are met. She is focused on speaking blessings to her husband and children, to make sure they are encouraged. She pursues the goals that God has given her in conjunction with making the home a central place and a refuge for the family.

(As a side note: please, abandon leisure clothing and sleepwear that is not enticing to your spouse. You may find that he will even be more romantic if you take that step toward him!)

Now, some words about communication. Men should provide more details for their wives to keep wives from asking a litany of questions. And women should reduce the number of words they use to communicate with their husbands by at least 50 percent. Half a woman's words are perceived by men as unnecessary "puffery."

If you wish to know what a man really means, close your ears and read the message that is communicated by his body movements. Do not listen to a man's words—they are often very different from what he does. Alternatively, a woman's physical behavior is often "acting out" and it is generally best to attend to her words.

> **Marital Secret: It is fruitless and senseless to waste valuable time asking "why" a spouse behaved in some way. See it, believe it, accept it and live on despite it.**

These are words to the wise that will help you eliminate days, months and years of bewilderment and confusion, and save you hours of counseling or therapy.

Eight Ways Husbands Hurt Their Wives

Marriage is not a practical necessity or a cure-all for lust and loneliness. It is a precious relationship that needs tender, self-sacrificing care. It is a holy calling, this union between a man and a woman. Unfortunately, we forget that. Wives and husbands are equally guilty. First, let's look at some of the ways that husbands hurt their wives:

1. Not going out of his way to add romance to the relationship.

2. Frequent criticism with hostile voice tones and words that hurt.

3. Showing preference to others over her.

4. Not paying attention to her words and ideas and wanting to give a quick fix solution without probing.

5. Acting as if he is superior and she is inferior.

6. Not doing enough household chores.

7. Trying to explain her hurts instead of just trying to understand her feelings, giving meanings to her statements that she did not intend.

8. Putting his needs and desires always before hers.

A loving husband will care for his wife in ways that will make her strong. He will be willing to sacrifice everything for her. Other than God, he should make her well-being his primary concern. He should care for her as he cares for his own body (see Ephesians 5:25-33 KJV).

Eight Ways Wives Hurt Their Husbands

Wives will not be fruitful by "preaching" to unbelieving, unequally yoked and/or incompatible husbands. A wife will be more successful in seeing a change in her husband by exhibiting the very behavior that she is requesting. Wives should practice what they want to preach and give life to their words by example. Here are some of the ways that wives hurt their husbands:

1. Asking for his advice, then ridiculing or not taking it. That doesn't encourage him to give his opinions in the future.

2. Wanting what he cannot give her and letting him know in some way that he is inadequate by negative facial expressions, body language and words that hurt.

3. Threatening to separate, divorce or withhold sex from him if he doesn't change.

4. Giving him in a negative or condescending way instructions on how to please her.

5. Constantly nagging.

6. Constantly criticizing and showing dissatisfaction with whatever he does and giving the impression that he can't do anything right.

7. Letting him know nonverbally that something is wrong yet denying anything is wrong when he asks.

8. Unfavorably comparing him to other men which may include former spouses, ex-boyfriends, her father, her brothers, or his best friends.

A wife must see to it that she deeply respects her husband, praising and honoring him. A wife must submit to her husband's leadership in the same way she submits to the Lord. Submission does not mean becoming a doormat, but means willingly following her husband's leadership in Christ.

We should distinguish submission from roles in the relationship. Roles in a marriage should be determined by each person's spiritual and motivational gifts. That may mean assigning nontraditional roles to either spouse. The wife may be responsible for handling the money and cutting the grass, while the husband may teach the children more or wash and iron the clothes. Be sure to agree on responsibilities based on the gifts and talents of the individual, not on family or societal traditions or expectations. Yes, husbands can look good in yellow rubber Playtex gloves!

Remember that marital problems are like storms. Storms do not come to stay, but we have to dwell in the midst of the storm in order to correct the problem. Recall Nahum 1:3 (NLT): "The Lord is slow to anger and great in power; the Lord will not leave the guilty unpunished. His way is in the whirlwind and the storm; and clouds are the dust of his feet." God will help you find the way out of each of your marital storms. But He needs each partner's spirit to stay focused, loving, joyful, patient, kind, good, faithful, gentle, centered, peaceful, self-controlled, calm and submitted to Him.

Chapter Four
Sustaining the Relationship

All of us are going to change after we get married. Marriage is the *beginning* of a long spiritual evolution together, not the end. Let us examine how maturity, growth and change should occur in a healthy and loving relationship.

Assume that the husband is the head of the family. As we study his footsteps, imagine that the husband is stepping forward in life with his right (righteous) foot and his wife is standing on his right side. Visualize the wife following him by placing her left foot directly in his footprint. They are walking through life together, and even though the husband may change his direction, the wife is right there, experiencing the change with her husband. If the husband and wife are stepping together, they will change together, and they will continue to be on one accord through each phase and transition in life. So the husband is changing and the wife is changing, and they're still in harmony with each other.

What does that mean? When one spouse steps to the "outside"—in conflict with the pre-marital promises and marital covenant—then the other partner should lovingly and prayerfully confront the departing spouse about their conduct and direction and keep them centered and focused on the goals, objectives, mission and purpose of the marriage. Keep this in mind: the husband's left foot and the wife's right foot are free members of their bodies; they represent individualism. However, those extensions of their individual selves remain dependent on the body—dependent on the marriage that nourishes and supports each spouse.

The success of a marriage depends largely on the degree to which each partner can demonstrate a genuine "open spirit." To do this, it will be important to discover what a closed spirit is. Here are the signs:

Five Signs of a Closed Spirit

A closed spirit is death to a marriage. It erects a wall of resistance and silence, cutting off communications, resulting in frustration and distress. Here are the tell-tale signs:

- Decrease in romance, physical contact, and frequency of sexual intercourse.

- Argumentative attitude.

- Resistance to discuss or agree on anything.

- Decline in asking for/respecting mate's advice.

- Finding ways to avoid each other.

As spouses and as lovers we should break down the barriers—the walls of silence—that separate us from our partners. We must not rely on our flesh and our feelings to motivate us to start communicating with our spouse. Instead we should immediately move toward actions that produce reconciliation, understanding that positive feelings and thoughts will follow later. Act right and then you'll *feel* right. Act right and then you'll *think* right.

Six Ways Husbands and Wives Can Open Their Spirits

To free and unseal the spirit of your spouse, it is important to be faithful to each other and protect each other's reputation, ego and integrity. Don't take each other too seriously and learn how to transform arguments and bad times into humor and lightheartedness. Learn each other's personal temperament, spirit and personal characteristics to help resolve conflict and restore your marriage. Consider these additional ways to open the spirit of communication, forgiveness and reconciliation with your spouse:

- Honor your mate; treat them as valuable. The healing humor of marriage is much more possible when each partner feels genuinely honored.

- Verbal and non-verbal communication with your spouse must come from the heart, and it cannot be faked.

- Ask for forgiveness and show consistent and progressive efforts to eliminate the problematic behavior.

- Exhibit a kind and gentle spirit toward your mate; give lots of gentle touches throughout each day; praise, affirm and edify each other.

- Do your best to understand what your mate has gone through before they married you and learn how to listen to and respect their thoughts and feelings, whether you believe they are valid or not.

- If your mate does become angry with you, acknowledge that they are hurting and admit you have given offense.

The Breath of Forgiveness

The breath of forgiveness is needed in marriages. Some people breathe easily; others require a greater effort. It all depends on the amount of oxygen their bodies are able to take in.

Normal breathing is silent. Difficult breathing—like difficulty with forgiving—is accompanied by obvious facial and body muscle strain as well as feelings of distress. You must take in the "deep breaths" of forgiveness. You must expand your faith—your lung capacity—by *inhaling* the peace of God and *exhaling* grace and mercy on your spouse who has offended you. Do this frequently—daily if necessary. "Forbear one another, and forgive one another, even as Christ forgave you" (Colossians 3:13 KJV).

Our breath of forgiveness must be a life style, and it must be done quickly, swiftly and easily, just as Jesus' breath of forgiveness refreshes us daily. Forgiveness in marriage is the daily and constant exchange of grace and mercy between spouses. In marriage, you can decide to be weak and hold onto the memory of pain and hurt feelings or you can become self-empowered and hold on to the marriage. Keep a short memory and forgive your spouse for even minor irritants. And remember—a righteous person will accept the apology of another regardless of the intensity of the offense.

> **Marital Secret: It is important to keep your heart clean by putting minor as well as major irritants, frustrations and offenses behind you.**

Does that seem weak? We, as members of the human race, dislike weakness. But it is in our weakness that God can be made strong in our lives (see II Corinthians 12:9). Instead of seeing forgiveness as weak, redefine weakness to mean your *inability* to release your true spirit, soul, righteous thoughts and nourishing emotions into the life of your mate. For what you focus on—what you think about—will empower you and either strengthen or break your strongholds of weakness.

It is often easy for us to have compassion for those who are born with a disadvantage, disability or weakness. However, our sense of compassion does not appear to transfer to those who are born strong and healthy and later become weak in character. Forgiveness is empowering and capable of changing you into a person who resembles Christ. Forgiveness is power. It is the core of reconciliation. Forgiveness is capable of bringing forth spiritual freedom, inner peace, and a healing of your own emotional wounds. It renews your integrity, mind and thoughts. Forgiveness is first for your benefit and secondly for your spouse. Forgiving others will enhance your relationship with God.

Many spouses fail to embrace the breath of forgiveness because they are protective of their own ego and afraid of being seen as vulnerable. Often they fail to forgive because of their miseducation about forgiveness. Forgiveness is an intellectual decision and not an emotional one. The Word of God requires it (see Matthew 6:14-15).

Forgiveness today doesn't mean that the offender won't re-create the same circumstances that could hurt us tomorrow. Nor does it mean that the offended can readily forget the hurt. Forgiveness also doesn't mean that the offending spouse should not be held responsible for the consequences of their behavior. Forgiving someone does not mean that we endorse their misconduct, nor does it mean that we can or should forget the details of the incident that harmed us. Forgiveness is merely casting the hurt away, dissolving the anger, irritation and frustration. And it does not preclude an ability to take practical precautions, if necessary, against repeated offenses.

There is a truth process to honor in effective communication and confrontation. First, it is important to understand the difference between opinion and fact. A lie is that which is contradicted by observable, provable facts; whereas it is possible for two people to have differing opinions, both supported by sound principles. It is important that we are honest with ourselves and distinguish fact versus personal opinion.

Second, after knowing what is the truth, then we should know what should be the healthy emotional response to that truth. Our judgments on marital issues should be based on the truth and couched with wisdom, grace and mercy. Our marital situations will change and improve when we learn how to change our perception and our point of view of the problem. When we choose wisely how we will feel and think about the circumstances, then the circumstances will have a chance to change for the better. The positive change must be internal first, and then positive changes will manifest themselves externally in what we call behavior.

Third, a healthy and appropriate emotional response is possible if there is a full hearing of the matter first which means being slow to take offense, speaking slowly, and being eager to hear the thoughts of your partner.

Fourth, having now bridled your tongue and having restrained yourself in order to hear and listen to your partner, it is crucial that you be flexible and insightful. Determine if your mate's behavior is worth the battle to seek a sincere apology, repentance and correction. Remember that in marriage it is best to be selective about your battles because there will be daily and often numerous aggravations between marital partners whether or not the couple is equally yoked.

Fifth, when the facts substantiate that you've been injured, and there is no justification for the offending action, then identify your hurt and ask for and expect an apology, repentance and correction from your partner.

Sixth, wrongdoers should identify, repent and recognize the impact that their wrong behavior had on their marital partner and/or be prepared to suffer the consequences of their offensive behavior.

Finally, the injured partner should acknowledge the wrongdoer's apology and repentance and understand how their partner was "glazed" by their family and personal histories. They should have realistic expectations of their partner's future behavior. The injured partner should forgive the repenting partner, even if it is for a repeated offense—just as Christ forgives us.

This approach to forgiveness is possible if we have reasonable expectations of our spouse, have set realistic boundaries in the marriage, and we respect the personality characteristics of our partner. We should pray for a spouse who offends us. We should respond to our spouse's acts and not react to the feelings invoked within us by those acts, nor should we attack the spouse's person. Remember that the offense represents only one point in time and not your spouse's whole lifetime. React only to the behavior of the moment.

Consequences of Not Forgiving

The consequences of not forgiving outweigh any emotional satisfaction we may gain by holding on to our grievances. They include growing resentment; harsh, vindictive behavior; alienation; and the feeling of being "locked" in a bad marriage. Contrast that with the blessings of breathing forgiveness: a sense of righteousness, calm and serenity, the ability to experience agape love, and true liberation of spirit.

It is important to remember once again that men and women are different, even when it comes to forgiving. Women typically have a need to hear from the man that he knows he was wrong. Most women want their men to humble themselves and exhibit verbal and physical signs of repentance. Men usually resist being broken down this way. They fail to understand that a simple "I'm sorry" does not necessarily indicate repentance. Repentance in marriage means being sorry enough—regretful enough—not to repeat the wrong behavior again. We all need to verbalize our apologies to each other. We all need to confess our sins, ask for forgiveness, and repent.

For the liberation of our own spirits, for peace of mind, and for wholeness, we must blow the breath of forgiveness on our spouse whether or not they recognize their offenses. We must be righteous despite the evil about us. We must forgive them—because we chose them—and we must patiently work with them in order to achieve compatibility, reconciliation and marital contentment.

Setting Acceptable Relationship Goals

The Finner-Williams Setting Relationship Goals Exercise Form is used to help couples identify problems and begin to set some acceptable boundaries, behaviors, activities and goals within the marriage. The **first** column is designed to identify problems. If something is causing either partner to think, act, or feel in a less-than-desirable way to the other partner, then it is a problem. If it is a source of irritation or frustration, then it is a problem.

The **second** column is designed to identify the ideal resolution to the problem. Often partners cannot agree on the ideal, perfect or ultimate resolution. If so, then in the **third** column the partners should enter their compromise or acceptable resolution to the problem. Partners with significant discord may not be able to agree on a compromise or acceptable resolution. This is when marital counseling, Christian counseling or marital therapy is recommended. The **fourth** column is designed to prioritize the problems. This form can be used by a couple in the privacy of their own home or in a treatment setting.

SETTING RELATIONSHIP GOALS EXERCISE			
IDENTIFIED PROBLEM	IDEAL	ACCEPTABLE	PRIORITY NUMBER

Date of Completion_____ Page____ of _____

Name of Preparer _____

Depending on their ability to work constructively together, the partners can complete the forms individually or as a couple.

There are a few common threads we have identified using this effective problem-solving tool. Be mindful that when you marry, you inherit your mate's relatives and friends. Couples who have benefited most from this exercise have learned that they should...

- Establish a bottom line in marriage without an option. For example, the bottom line could be that divorce is not an option and that you will remain together despite all that may happen.

- Use lovemaking as a cleansing and healing process, even if there are arguments and fights. When lovemaking stops, there may be arguments, cheating, and emotional or physical abuse. Lovemaking is important and through that process a cleansing occurs, and a healing of the spiritual wound can take place. Pay special attention during this time to talk and engage in sensual touching.

- Accept their partners without anticipation of changes and improvements. It is common to have a tendency to want to change your partner. There is a tendency to want to make your partner over. Forget about it. It's not going to work. To borrow a coined phrase, what you see is what you get.

- Negotiate for time and space in the home, and take it. Sometimes you may need personal time and space away from your spouse or others. You should ask for the time out, be specific about the time span needed, and tell how you will utilize the time. Don't expect the partner to know that you need the time out or to know how long you will be absent.

- Stick to the agreed upon time out-period. If more time is needed, it is only appropriate to re-negotiate the time span and to obtain mutual agreement with limitations.

- Establish an irrevocable day and time during the week or weekend to have a family meeting with your partner to discuss issues relative to finances, marital assets, personal calendars, children, obligations, responsibilities, feelings, thoughts, etc.

- Cry only for a reason and only for a short season. Then change or eliminate whatever causes you to cry. Stop crying as soon as possible.

- Never leave the marital home in the midst of an argument. Instead, designate areas that each partner can retreat to until emotions are more stable. Remember, if you leave the home during arguments, you are more likely to separate. If you separate from each other, then you are more likely to divorce. And, if you divorce, you will be alone and subject to remarrying someone similar to your current spouse if you did not learn how and why you made poor choices in the present marriage.

- Plan how to manage finances. Money can be a problem; it affects many other aspects of life. Whoever manages the money best (not necessarily who makes the most money) should be allowed to do so. Making more money isn't necessarily equivalent with good money management skills. Usually, there are problems or issues when the wife makes more money than her husband. Women in such positions need to honor their husbands—their earthly kings. And men in such positions need to feel secure about their favor with their wife and with God, and in their headship of the marriage regardless of their income. Men and women who are led by God are willing to walk side by side together in order to fulfill the Master's plan for their marriage and their individual lives.

Often when newlyweds seek marital counseling, prioritizing of the household bills is presented as a common problem. We utilize the Setting Acceptable Relationship Goals Form in order to achieve an acceptable order of payments. "The Finner-Williams Debt Payment Decision Making Game" process was created from these experiences. Let's look at a typical monthly bill profile:

- Automobile Insurance (30 days past due)
- Water Bill (current)
- Cable Service (current)
- Electric Bill (current)
- Credit Card (current)
- Movies (entertainment)
- Restaurant
- Department Store Card (30 days past due)
- House Insurance (current)
- House Mortgage (current)
- Life Insurance (current)
- Credit Card (60 days past due)
- Gas Credit Card (60 days past due)
- Clothing
- Food
- Make-up, Hair and Nail Services
- Video Games (Entertainment)
- Long Distance Service
- Telephone Bill (30 days past due)
- Credit Card (90 days past due)

Clients are asked to prioritize these debts in order of importance. We interviewed ten mature and financially successful couples and asked them to take these bills, prioritize them and provide us with the rationale for their listing. (The detailed rationale is published in our "Debt Game.") Here is what the couples suggested:

1. House Mortgage

2. House Insurance

3. Water

4. Electric

5. Gas

6. Life Insurance

7. Automobile Payment

8. Automobile Insurance

9. Major Credit Card

10. Gas Credit Card

11. Major Credit Card

12. Store Credit Card

13. Store Credit Card

14. Telephone Service

15. Major Credit Card

16. Cable Service

17. Long Distance Telephone Bill

18. Food

19. Make-up, Hair and Nail Services

20. Clothing

21. Movies (entertainment)

22. Rental of Video Games (entertainment)

23. Restaurant Dinner

Another common problem is when there is an unhealthy and damaging socio-economic difference between the husband and wife. Usually the problem exists when the wife makes more money than the husband. The "Setting Relationship Goals Exercise Form" process has assisted couples from different socio-economic backgrounds. These are important understandings to embrace:

- It is a blessing and advantage to not be under pressure to work a second job in order to bring in more money.

- Differences in money and educational degrees are not important.

- Money and degrees are a means toward an end and not the ultimate goal.

- The income earned by both parties should be counted as one total income, not two separate incomes.

- There can be a healthy way to handle the situation when the husband and wife share the same value systems.

- The one making less money is not less of a person.

The way that we love God is indicative of the way that we will love our spouse. Couples must remain willing to break strongholds and eliminate barriers that separate their spirits and flesh from each other. This means being motivated to change—motivated to become new creatures and put aside the behaviors, emotions and thoughts that delay reconciliation and renewal of the marital covenant.

Factors for A Successful God-Centered Marriage

Most importantly, God must always be the guiding force in married partners' lives and in the home. Proverbs 11:29 (KJV) tells us, "He that troubleth his own house shall inherit the wind and the fool shall be servant to the wise of heart." Partners must allow God to emerge as the leader and the head of the relationship. This will eliminate the struggle over who is the head or leader of the marriage. There are several important factors to consider in improving Christian marital relationships:

Partnership promotes harmony and shared interest in the marriage. Partnership eliminates the struggle and warfare of who is truly in charge of the marriage. It encourages spouses to work together not only to resolve differences but to share equal responsibility for the happiness and success of the relationship. It rids spouses of the tension and stress caused often by one dominating over another in the marriage. It promotes oneness and equality, not separateness (what's mine or what's yours).

Husbands often quote the Scripture, "... the husband is the head of the wife, even as Christ is the head of the church; and the savior of the body" (Ephesians 5:23 KJV). However, what about "A wise man will hear, and will increase learning, and a man of understanding shall attain unto wise counsel" (Proverbs 1:5 KJV)? Husbands sometimes fail to recognize that their wives are wise counsels. A husband who is an effective head of the home will recognize, respect and consider his wife's wise counsel.

Friendship is very important in marriage. If spouses can be friends with one another like they choose to be with others, their relationships will improve tremendously. Friendship is practiced throughout each day by the sharing of pleasures, joys, disappointments, needs, ideas and concerns. It creates a sense of caring, intimacy, and love. Friendship often provides the nurture in marriage that inspires spouses to communicate and interact with one another freely. Husbands should be their wives' best "girlfriends" and wives should be their husbands' closest friends and "homeboys."

Worship is very important. Spouses who worship together are likely to stay together because God will intervene in their lives at the same time. Spouses must worship together not only when they attend church on Sundays, but also during the week, at home and on their jobs. Couples that walk together in the same footprints of life cannot drift apart.

Prayer is the single most important factor that rids spouses of burdens and yokes caused by stress in their lives. Spouses should pray together "out loud" when they are together, and throughout the day for each other when they are apart. We recommend that spouses pray about their challenges and concerns. The entire family should pray out loud together as often as possible.

Love is the essence of keeping the marriage strong, happy and free of continuous problems. Married partners must love one another as they love God in order to honor their commitment to one another. Love, like marriage, is not easy to obtain. Spouses must work, work, and work at improving their relationship. The work can become simple, easy and fun when God is involved in each spouse's life and relationship. Try loving one another as you love God in an effort to improve your marriage and relationship.

Humor between a wife and husband is psycho-spiritual food. Both parties should acquire the ability to perceive, enjoy and express their respective judgments or opinions about marital problems in a humorous manner. This will release the tension, the feelings of desperation, the fear and the suspicion that is often associated with the common problems and human struggles we encounter when living with another adult.

Dating your spouse on a regular weekly or bi-weekly schedule will provide a couple with the quality time needed to attend to each other's emotional needs. This special forum will give couples an opportunity to establish the prolonged, direct eye-to-eye contact and uninterrupted conversation that we miss in the hustle and bustle of everyday life. Eyes are the reflections of our souls and spirits. During the social outing or marital date, we suggest that you stare into each other's eyes and examine each other's faces with loving intensity.

Intimacy is so important. Our empirical research reveals that husbands and wives that submit to each other's flesh at least once every 72 hours communicate best with each other. "Do not deprive each other except by mutual consent and for a time, so that you may devote yourselves to prayer. Then come together again so that Satan will not tempt you because of your lack of self-control" (1 Corinthians 7:5 NIV).

Becoming One Spirit is essential. "So ought men to love their wives as their own bodies. He that loveth his wife loveth himself" (Ephesians 5:28 KJV). After marriage, each spouse must change their life style and mind-set from being a single, independent self-sufficient individual, to being "one body-one spirit in the grace of life" with one mutually agreeable marital mission and purpose that each party can articulate to the world without reservation or hesitation. "Likewise, ye husbands, dwell with them according to knowledge, giving honor unto the wife as unto the weaker vessel, and being heirs together of the grace of life, that your prayers be not hindered" (I Peter 3:7 KJV).

Techniques for Sustaining Healthy Romantic Relationships

When you are in a marriage, you need to meet the needs of your partner. You need to learn how to satisfy and relate to your mate. For those of you who like categorical lists of behaviors and suggestions, this section is for you.

In our society, and because of the way that we have been socialized, romance and sex are indeed a significant part of civil and covenant marriages. When you hear a male or female say romance or sex is not important, it is usually not the truth and it is their defense to the dissatisfaction they may be having in their marital romance or sexual life. If you are not satisfied with your marriage, ask yourself the following questions:

Am I...

- being careful to avoid any thoughts of jealously, suspicion or distrust?

- actively participating in family events and including family members in weekly family discussions in the home?

- giving and insisting upon mutual respect among all family members?

- aggressively seeking to eliminate or prevent all crime, violence, drug use or abuse of any kind in my home?

- going out of my way to add romance to my spouse's life?

- paying careful attention to the traps and patterns that have caused trouble in the past?

- developing immediate (next twelve months) and long-range (next five years) goals in terms of my spiritual, family, financial, mental, social and physical life? Do I have a time table for my goals and a plan to monitor progress?

- always learning about my spouse?

- letting my spouse know verbally when something is wrong, instead of displaying negative attitudes or body language?

- displaying romance as much as possible, complete with kind and loving gifts such as massages, favorite meals, intimate presents, surprises, etc.?

The following specific activities should assist with sustaining healthy, romantic marriages:

- Be honest about your relationships with other persons. Have full disclosure about all relationships with females and males.

- Agree on how the two of you will relate to each others' family members, friends, former lovers and others.

- Have a zero tolerance level for adultery and any abuse by either party.

- Don't accept your current situation as being your final situation; expect that those temporary and temporal things will change.

- Except in the cases of abuse and a few other biblically-based exceptions, view separation and divorce as no options to a marital problem.

- Allow your roles and responsibilities to change and make gracious transitions as life conditions so dictate.

- Socialize with in-laws, children, friends, co-workers, etc., together instead of separately.

- Identify those areas in your life that need to be healed and get assistance or support to heal and bind all of those open wounds.

- Learn to enjoy your own personal company without the closeness of intimacy with another person. Refuse to surrender to the feelings of desperation and loneliness.

- Maintain a lifestyle that can easily be supported by one income, and avoid taking on heavy financial commitments.

- Don't socialize with single friends of the opposite sex who despise their singleness and want to get married.

The Spiritual Dance of a Man and a Woman

> **Marital Secret: The state of your spirit determines the quality of your marriage.**

Spirituality is the breath of life. Your spirituality affects the way you relate to and regard others, God and the world around you. We bring our spirits to everything that we do. When God speaks, He speaks to our spirits. Our spirits determine how we respond, react, cope with and handle victories, defeats, and life-changing events.

We talked about open and closed spirits. Picture this: open spirits in a dance of joy. Why are they dancing?

They are dancing because they have learned to humble themselves. The Book of James says, "God resists the proud, but gives grace to the humble" (James 4:6 KJV). Humility ignites the spirit of man and woman, causing it to burn radiantly forever. Humility is meek, not weak, as some people misinterpret it. The quality is borne out of one who has first submitted to God. It serves as a catalyst for spiritual growth and development throughout life.

A humble person attracts gracious responses like a magnet. Admit it—isn't your heart warmed by a humble person? Isn't it hard to get angry at a truly humble individual? Just think how powerful a relationship can be when both parties are humble. Talk about "warm hearts, warm beds!"

Humility is what sustains relationships during periods of unwillingness to forgive, disappointment, mistrust, dishonesty, and other difficulties. And humility paves the way for genuine love: the kind of love that results in compassion and tenderness; the kind of love that extinguishes conflict; the kind of love that bonds people together, causing much personal growth, fulfillment and happiness.

Humility leads us into love, and for the Christian the inevitable result is prayer. Prayer is essential in the spiritual "dance." Prayer gives resources, strength and energy. It is the gateway to wisdom about God and about each other. It is spiritual cover or protection against evil invaders—human or spiritual.

Humility and love allow us to freely and genuinely display the "fruit of the Spirit" (Galatians 5:22 KJV): love, joy, peace, long suffering, gentleness, goodness, faith, meekness and temperance. They keep us from frustration and hostility, belligerence and revenge, anxiety and fear. Once the fruit grows in the soil of humility and love, it will show on your face, radiate in your eyes and exhibit itself in the graciousness of your speech.

The mental, intellectual and emotional energies in you that motivate you to move so that you can perform at a higher level of functioning are what we call your psychospirituality (others may can it your spirit). Psychospirituality gives life to physical organisms; it determines to what degree a person has a zestful or brisk quality in their approach to life. It is a person's mood, nature, and frame of mind. Your spirit is your personal fire—your personal internal flame. It is important to not let your flame die, for the illumination of its light is the only way that people can follow the pathway to the true you. The spirit of a person is the true essence of their existence.

What is important here is consistency. Your spouse needs to know and be able to anticipate who you are from day to day. That doesn't mean you'll never have a bad day. It does mean that, in general, your overall demeanor, attitude and actions will manifest the "spiritual fruits." Spiritually consistent spouses are equally yoked and compatible.

What is one of the most dangerous barriers to compatibility? Self-pity. Self-pity affects motivation and attitude. It can poison our relationships with our partners, spouses and others. We should speak against such unclean spirits and demons with authority! These attitude "demons" confronted Jesus, so you know that they will attack if you allow them to. Make sure that in all your guarding, you guard yourself against this destructive emotion.

You have the spiritual power to choose your perspective and attitude. You must be spiritually sensitive to God so that you can bless your spouse with your life, with the truth and as you want to be blessed. What you invest in your marriage will show in your spirit. It is in the spirit that we can resolve any problem or situation.

A spiritual marriage allows movement and freedom, enabling a couple to stretch and grow together as they work out their respective roles and plan together for the future. The closer we move toward humility and love, the freer we are from the gravity of the flesh. The happy result? Marriage becomes the purifying vessel that perfects our characters.

As princes and princesses of our heavenly Father, we must stand firm on the foundation of our faith and the promises of God so that the beautiful spirit that he has given us will shine on the outside of our faces and coat our tongues with words of peace, praise and glory. We are a mighty and peculiar people, and we must always remember that we already have an inherited claim to the many promises of God.

The Art of Submission

We want to share with you a personal testimony:

It was pretty snazzy, my 1982 triple-black Cadillac Eldorado Biarritz with a red racer stripe. I fondly named her "The Black Beauty." One could use similar language and terms to describe "The Black Beauty" and me. Black Beauty had character, pride, distinction, and she was sharply tailored. It had style and grace with an all-business instrumentation. This automobile was known for its ability to tailor to the environment and adjust with fingertip controls. As a proud single woman I was distinguished and known to have a bold character. I always knew exactly where I was going, and I got there on my own terms. I had a keen sense of my rights and privileges as well as my duties, obligations and responsibilities. I was sharply tailored, gracious and I had style. I was serious about any and all jobs that I engaged. Though flexible and adaptable, I insisted on being in control at all times. It was either "my way or the highway." I was the climate controller—I controlled the circumstances in each area of my life. And I would never settle for less—that's why I chose the Cadillac Eldorado Biarritz, the most sought after collectible automobile of its era.

When Robert Dee Williams and I married, The Black Beauty was six years old and I continued to drive her. When Black Beauty was 13 years old, a marital decision was made to lease a Lincoln. Regardless of costly repairs, new parts and major restoration effects, the Black Beauty had lost much of her bold power, flexibility and control. She no longer was easy to handle, and her performance became sluggish and unpredictable. Black Beauty's fire and efficiency were no more than a memory and we prayed that our angels would ward off the imminent danger of unexpected surprises on the road.

The security that once cradled me now betrayed me and left me feeling vulnerable. But she had not lost her snazzy style, condition and beauty. She remained a sought-after collectable, even in her mature years. I could only pray that mounting years and maturity would be as kind to me.

Robert began to drive Black Beauty. Often we would drive to work together in our separate cars. Initially, driving the Lincoln Continental, I would precede the Black Beauty as we traveled home from our office parking lot. This was most difficult, frustrating and irritating. The Black Beauty could barely move above 30 miles per hour without shaking. She would not make the same lights as the Lincoln. She would lose her power, fall back, and cause an increased distance between Rob and me. Black Beauty's noise was a nuisance. I found myself constantly looking in the rear view mirror and wondering what my husband was doing and why he couldn't move faster. It was difficult to see Rob, and it was difficult to measure the actual distance between our automobiles.

One day, the Lord whispered to me and told me to let Robert precede me with Black Beauty. The benefit was for me to know how to aid and assist him— how to meet the needs of my husband in the event of his experiencing problems with our older automobile. It took some time to adapt to the change. In the beginning, there were a few incidents of relapse as I resumed the old practice of driving out of the parking lot before Rob. However, when I came to myself, I pulled into the parking lane, allowing my husband to regain his rightful position as the lead automobile.

After a few weeks, our drives brought me several unanticipated benefits. Keeping my eyes focused ahead on Black Beauty and my husband didn't require as much intense concentration as watching him through the rear view mirror. It allowed me to wind down from my long work day and actually hear the words of the gospel music I played. My husband took his leadership position seriously. He obeyed all traffic laws to make sure that the police didn't stop him, and therefore they wouldn't stop me.

Letting my husband take the lead afforded me an opportunity to make mental plans for the next business day and deliberate on the blessings and losses of the present day. Letting my husband lead allowed me to remain at peace, knowing that he would study the road and guard both of us and keep us out of harm's way. My husband kept at least three car lengths behind any obstacle in front of us, so if Rob was safe, I was safe. My acquiescence to my husband taught me to trust and respect him despite his faults. My yielding to Rob day after day, week after week, year after year showed me his driving patterns and his decision-making process. My deferring to the will and direction of my husband eventually taught me his personal style for successfully maneuvering and handling the unexpected detours, road construction, closed lanes and barriers in the road of life.

In time I learned to expect and not be insulted by his checking my gas meter each morning as he kissed me goodbye. I learned not to be offended when he drove into the garage first to assure my safety and protection. My looking to him to lead us in Black Beauty was the manifestation of my respect, my free-will submission and my love for my husband.

It may be easier for women to accept the "S" word (submission) if we examine its components closer and from a different perspective. The word submission can be separated into two parts. The first part is "sub" or to come under, below, beneath or to be secondary. The second part of word is "mission" which means a self-imposed duty, principles of Christianity, afflicted care for and the supply of a need. As God-honoring wives, we are merely coming under the self-imposed marital duties and principles of Christianity in order to care for and meet the needs of our partner. Each couple needs to have a **mutually agreeable written marital mission statement.** Once again, here is ours:

The Marital Mission of Robert and Paris Williams

The mission of our marriage is to live a quality life together that is based on the Holy Bible and reflective of the personality, spirit and heart of Jesus Christ. It is our intent to enjoy the richness of agape and intimate love daily. The essence of our marriage is to have open, free and honest communications at all times and about all matters that affect our individual and collective, personal and professional lives. We shall view our marriage and our marital home as our refuge and sanctuary from the influences of this world. We shall safeguard the holy bonds of our covenant marriage, pledging that physical separation from each other and divorce shall never be options nor shall they be subjects for discussion. It is our commission to love, honor and respect each other and regard each other as top priorities, second only to our Lord and Savior Jesus Christ. It is our duty to seek mutual agreement on all matters, and to delegate and make assignment of responsibilities based on our individual gifts and motivations. And it is our unified purpose to daily worship and praise the Lord together, to honor God's will and to abide by the biblical requirements for husbands, wives and marriage.

Following Black Beauty in the Lincoln Continental gave me a new perspective on my husband. I took note that Rob always wore his seat belt. He always slowed down and stopped for amber lights instead of rushing through them, so that we stayed together. Eventually, I began to see Rob as both gracious and bold. He became more efficient, in charge and able to control our marital affairs. My faith in his directing us safely taught me that he would be responsive in any and every surprise event, emergency and unexpected problem in our life together. He communicated carefully and effectively with me by using his turn signal, and giving me a sign in the mirror that all was "OK."

To be subjected to your husband means to die to self-will for your husband. A cheerful and loving submission is an effective way to win unbelieving husbands to salvation—and to edify Christian husbands, further nourishing their Christian growth. Mark 10:43-44 (KJV) tells us that whoever desires to be great among you must be a servant. Husbands and wives are partners in receiving God's blessings. Husbands and wives are expected to attend to their marital business together and to honor their diversity and differences. Husbands and wives are to be servants to one another and to develop their capacity to serve one another. We should submit our individual selves to one another—to one united flame of life. Let us aim for and eagerly pursue what makes for harmony and for mutual edification and development of one another (Romans 14:19 KJV Amplified) in marriage.

Recently we donated Black Beauty to a charity and bought a Mercury Sable to take her place. It was an emotional experience for me—Black Beauty and I had 17 years together. Both automobiles have character, sharp design, grace, style, control, boldness, power and easy handling. Our spiritual and biblical lessons were well learned. Despite our individual growth and development, maturing and the change in our circumstances, the Lincoln Continental now joyfully submits to the Mercury Sable. It's God's speed.

Chapter Five
Sex

Good lovemaking and good sexual intercourse are spiritual experiences. Each is like a spiritual dance between partners. There are basically three kinds of lovemaking: (1) quick lovemaking, (2) stress release lovemaking, and the (3) "covenant romantic spiritual dance" lovemaking. Lovemaking is like competitive ice skating programs; there are short programs and there are long programs. Each couple should determine their own personal lovemaking needs and adjust accordingly. Like ice skating, each encounter should have some basic elements and requirements that will bring each partner satisfaction.

Warm Hearts—Cold Beds

Intimacy can be either sexual or non-sexual. Good old-fashioned romantic covenant lovemaking is a transforming experience. However, many people don't have the time or energy to pursue the transformation. Partners usually want to please their spouse, but sometimes there are problems. Warm hearts but cold beds prevail in the face of medical problems, loss of sexual desire, pain during intercourse, inability to achieve an erection, or stress that arises from multiple roles and responsibilities. These psychological stressors stem from work, home, the core or extended family, community and church.

It is important to whittle down multiple demands. Minimize the balls of responsibilities in life that you juggle. Get others to assist you—it may be your spouse, child, family member, in-law, church member, co-worker or committee member. Concentrate on doing those things that are consistent with your spiritual and motivational gifts, and delegate the rest away as much as possible. Next, it is important that you learn how to assert a gracious "No" to requests made on your time or for your involvement—particularly when your plate is full and the request is not consistent with your spiritual gifts. For example, if exhortation is not your motivational gift, then perhaps you should not be in the counseling ministry. If teaching is not your natural God-given gift, then perhaps you shouldn't be completing credits to satisfy the requirements for a teaching certificate.

In order for frigidity and cold beds to be eliminated in the face of the challenging dual career family, it is important that conflicts or confusion about male and female roles and responsibilities in the family are redesigned and resolved. This can be achieved by (1) reorganizing your routines, (2) getting up earlier, (3) getting sufficient sleep, (4) choosing among essential commitments, (5) resolving money problems in the marriage, (6) avoiding the non-essentials, (7) lowering your standards and demands for perfection, (8) not feeling guilty about what you can't accomplish, and (9) prioritizing your roles and responsibilities in order of spouse, parent, compensated worker, relative, person and friend.

Finally, understand that it is important to perceive lovemaking and sexual intercourse with your spouse as gifts to yourself and not merely as other duties in the institution of marriage. This "duty" attitude leads to disastrous consequences, such as using lovemaking as a form of reward or punishment. Often those who employ such manipulations are those who don't enjoy sex or who don't agree with their partner about the desired frequency of lovemaking.

We should let go of certain negative thoughts and beliefs in due time and in due season. To rehabilitate the lack of interest in sex, we encourage you to try the following techniques that have proven effective with some of our marital couples:

- Schedule lovemaking if you have to, to avoid falling into a dangerous pattern of separation. Forget all obligations and responsibilities, and focus on touch.

- Have a physical examination to assure that there are no medical explanations for your loss of interest in sex. Work closely with your physician to learn what medical procedures, medication regime, and/or surgical correction may improve your comfort level and ability to have satisfying sex with your spouse.

- Allow your senses to be free and give yourself permission to be sexually aroused.

- Take your partner's hand and put it where you need for it to be in order for you to experience pleasure.

- Don't view sex as merely the physical act of having sexual intercourse. It is not and should not be viewed as merely penetration of the penis into the vaginal canal. View making love as a spiritual dance between the partners who are using a different type of language to communicate with each other. View the lovemaking as a mutual gift that will allow spouses to come away from the experience feeling more satisfied, transformed to a higher plane and more spiritually in-tune with each other.

- Explore each other's bodies by lightly gliding your fingertips across the skin of your partner with the lights on and then without the lights on. This builds up anticipation for the next hand move.

- Couples need to remember that some people lose their sex drive if there is repeated mere physical sex (quick and stress release lovemaking) in lieu of the covenant romantic spiritual dance of love and sex. Maximize the latter.

- Vary the lovemaking program. When you stay with the same sexual positions, lovemaking can get boring and fail to stimulate. Discover new positions and movements together.

Above all, it is important that the partners talk about intimacy problems. It is important that there is appreciation for each person's opinions, feelings and needs.

Male Intimacy

In comparison to women, most men tend to see sex as more of a physical act than a romantic intimate act. However, women need to gain an appreciation for that physical forthright need of men. Once a wife gains appreciation for the reality of that physical perspective, then she will be able to allow herself to have some similar physically "forthright" days, too! Appreciating and responding to her husband's physical need will foster more romantic responses from him.

There are two sexual problems that most affect men: the lack of quality of the sexual act and impaired performance. These problems can be resolved. Men, recognize that if there is no apparent medical problem, then the mental issue is even more important than the performance issue. And to both men and women: do you know what physical actions (including verbal communication) most please your partner? Talk about it, then do it! There is much freedom that married couples can have here.

Healthy sexuality and satisfying sexual encounters will impact self-esteem and the ability of couples to communicate. Thus it is important to give each other positive feedback during the basking afterglow of the lovemaking. Avoid any negative feedback until both of you are out of the bedroom or lovemaking area.

Now, for some "rules of thumb." Foreplay is normally about 20 to 30 minutes during the "covenant romantic spiritual dance" lovemaking. Couples should verbally share their rich sexual fantasies during foreplay and during the sexual act. The frequency of lovemaking should be mutually agreed upon by both parties.

Couples that we counsel indicate that the husband desires sex at least once daily. Most men, when honest, report that they have a sexual thought at least once each and every conscious hour. The frequency of lovemaking often is an intimacy problem. We routinely ask clients in counseling how often they make love each week. Based on the hundreds of reports given by those couples who have been most successful in counseling and treatment, we have developed a rule of thumb. If there is not mutual agreement among the partners, it is our suggestion that a couple should make love at least once every two to three days (or once every 72 hours). We call this the "72 Hours Rule." After a certain time period, say six to nine months, the husband and wife should evaluate and adjust the frequency according to the needs of both partners. This will probably lead to a more reasonable and steady sexual relationship.

Sexual freedom is important. As a couple you should explore each other's bodies and learn where your partner's erogenous zones are located. In our "Enhancing Romantic Relationships Workshops," men tell us that their favorite erogenous zones are:

- the entire neck area

- behind the knees

- fingers taken through their hair

- kissing, fingertips, and soft fabric (e.g.; feathers, mink, silk, etc.) taken across their chest and nipples

- the entire ear surface and inner ear area

- lower back area

- surface of buttocks

This list is not all-inclusive; each man should communicate with their spouse by adding and subtracting from this list according to their individual sexuality. Our bodies change; we must remain in touch with our physical and sexual senses so that our spouses are kept abreast of what delights us. If partners are not satisfying each other and the result is negative behaviors such as abuse, infidelity, separation, or other self-defeating activities, marital and/or individual counseling should be considered.

However, men, when you follow the suggestions we have discussed for the purpose of enhancing your romantic relationship with your wife, then we are confident that you will be "richly rewarded" by your wife.

Female Intimacy

The miseducation of some women is that wives have a responsibility to give sexual pleasure and not to receive sexual pleasure. This can be a major barrier in marriage. Some women are not comfortable with their naked body or with their own sexuality, especially if they are small in stature, small breasted, full figured, or have a small pelvis.

Christian women need to understand, accept, and believe that it is all right for married women to have frequent, pleasurable, passionate lovemaking with their husbands and be multi-orgasmic. You can love God, your husband and sex simultaneously, and still be saved and go to heaven!

The following are some suggestions to consider. Women need to assume responsibility for their own sexual fulfillment and not wait for sex to happen to them. This starts by getting to know the details of your own body and the body of your spouse. In the context of a loving marriage, women and men should understand their bodies and learn what gives them pleasure. It can help men and women to become more comfortable with their own sexuality.

We are sure some of you will want us to clarify what we mean. We are not talking about a solo activity designed purely as a means to the end of self-pleasure. If sexual fulfillment is done for this purpose, it defeats the God-given goal of oneness in marriage and becomes a self-centered and marriage-defeating activity. If, however, it is done as part of the sexual relationship between a husband and wife, and both parties have agreed that this is desirable, such sexual activities can serve to educate the couple and enhance the marital bed.

Women tell us that their favorite erogenous zones are:

- the entire ear surface and inner ear

- breasts and nipples

- kissing on the toes and bottom of feet

- kissing in the palm of hands

- the inner thighs

And of course, there is the now-famous "G-spot." Although much has been written about the location and nature of this area of a woman's body, some women still don't know where it is or what it can do for them. Here is a short primer:

The G-spot is simply an area of spongy tissue located behind the pubic bone and around the urethra. By inserting two fingers into the vagina (approximately to the second joint) and stimulating the area, pressing fairly firmly and deeply if necessary, a woman can achieve an extremely intense orgasm. On the first occasions, there may be some discomfort or even the urge to urinate, but don't be afraid to keep trying as you continue to explore one another. Also, do not be surprised if fluid is ejected from the urethra itself—it is probably not urine, but a fluid that is produced in response to the woman's sexual excitation.

But sex is not just physiology. As most of you have learned, there is a mental component as well—even more important than the physical act. The following are some suggestions for how wives can improve their sexual lives:

- Have the mind set and spirit of wanting to meet your mate's needs.

- Instruct your sexual partner how to please you sexually with sufficient verbal details and practice.

- Be selective about statements that may provoke an argument. Approach lovemaking with a positive attitude and self-confidence.

- Enjoy your spouse and partner with all your body, soul and spirit!

- Be consistent with your emotions and feelings so that your partner can feel security in your reverence and character.

- Accept the fact that men have an intense sex drive. Most men report that they have a need to release their sexual drive every four to five days and that sex is your husband's way to connect with you.

- Understand that even if you aren't in the mood to make love, you can choose to feel differently and welcome the opportunity to make love.

- Plan romantic weekend(s) with several surprises for your partner.

- Create an atmosphere in your bedroom which will encourage good romance and good sex (i.e., no clothing on the floor, junk on the dresser, newspapers in the corner, etc.).

- Be aggressive, because men like a more physical approach to sex and lovemaking.

- Give your husband and partner what he wants with passion, romance and with a loving attitude. Break the negative yoke against the kind of submission that leads to passivity in lovemaking.

- Know that good lovemaking is within the plan of God, if done within the marital covenant. Know that sex is honorable, wholesome and healthy. God expects you to immerse yourself in your husband's love and embraces, and to continually delight in his body! (see Proverbs 5:15, 18-19 KJV)

Good sex should be associated with a woman's general well-being. When any one of the following issues are evident, then it is advisable that women should seek professional marital or individual counseling:

1. Evidence of or admission of extra-marital affairs.

2. Lack of communication/understanding.

3. Any kind of abuse (physical, mental, emotional, mental, etc.) by you or against you.

4. Physical and emotional abandonment by you or against you.

5. Inability to apologize to or forgive each other for your respective trespasses, sins and offenses against each other.

6. A pattern of omissions and/or lies by either partner.

Joy with Menopause

Menopause is the transitional phase in a woman's life when she experiences a decrease in estrogen and testosterone levels. There are several kinds of menopause and causes. Natural menopause occurs for most women between the ages of 48 and 55. The process can begin as early as 43, but more commonly between the ages of 48 and 50. If menopause happens before the age of 40, it is called premature. Artificial menopause happens because of surgery, radiation or drug treatments. Late menopause, which is rare, occurs at about 60 years of age.

Menopause, whether early or late, natural or artificial, carries with it significant physical, emotional and psychological implications. A full hormonal profile done by a competent physician can help women deal with the changes and challenges of menopause.

According to urologist Jennifer Berman, a hormonal profile should consist of:

• a full physical evaluation

• a psychosexual evaluation

• a physiologic evaluation

• measurements of genital blood flow, vaginal pH, genital sensation and vaginal elasticity

Alexis Pickens, Jr., M.D., SACOG, a practicing obstetrician and gynecologist in Detroit, Michigan, advises that women experiencing menopause

"...hold the key to their own health. They should be careful and ask their friends for a referral to an experienced and effective physician who is known to have the best interest of their female patients at heart. At this point in their life, they should be open and willing to aggressively seek competent help when they need it. *Think of the body as a vessel so that it will hold what life later pours into it.*" (emphasis ours)

As a natural product of aging, we know that life may pour into our vessels the following problems: osteoarthritis; cardiovascular diseases; thinning and graying of the hair; losses in muscle strength, hearing, taste, balance and voice; respiratory and heart problems; decrease in sexual desire; loss of bladder control... the list is endless!

Not much to look forward to, is it? To compound the matter, psychosexual symptoms of the premenstrual syndrome (PMS), perimenopause (the beginnings of menopause), and menopause are often similar, making women even more confused about their emotions, feelings and behavior. Husbands, know that your wife may at any time feel sad, irritable, tense, tired or fearful more than usual in response to typical daily irritations and frustrations. She may feel overwhelmed, forget things, have a major appetite change, or even hallucinate or have thoughts of suicide. All of these are within the range of normal reactions, but when more than seven of these symptoms are present consistently, a doctor's appointment is in order to determine whether there is an imbalance in the estrogen and testosterone levels.

Women, you can also expect hot flashes, or "private summers;" vaginal dryness and atrophy; decreased arousal and increased difficulty reaching orgasm.

But hope cometh! After seeking and following competent medical treatment, couples should be able to cope and handle menopause with humor and joy. Husbands, fan your wives during her "private summers"—she'll love you for it! There should be honest, open and free communication between partners. Wives, let your husband know when you are experiencing any of these symptoms; don't keep him guessing!

Here are some more suggestions for coping with menopause:

- Embrace and appreciate the fact that as a woman you (usually) no longer have to worry about becoming pregnant, nor do you need to be concerned whether your birth control method is effective.

- Enjoy the benefits of sexual freedom with your partner; such as spontaneous lovemaking in a wide variety of areas at home.

- According to Dr. Berman, discuss with your physician the feasibility of using a device called the Eros, which is a vacuum pump that helps promote blood flow to the clitoris. Also discuss the feasibility of hormonal therapy, diuretic drug therapy, vitamin therapy and medications that enhance smooth muscle relaxation such as apomorphine, phentolamine and prostaglandin.

- Learn relaxation techniques and stress management techniques.

- Make dietary changes in consultation with your physician.

- Exercise regularly.

- Increase the frequency of hugs and cradling—but not during episodes of hot flashes (private summers).

- Increase the length of foreplay.

- Get professional massages and ask your husband to give you a massage.

Wives should also conduct Kegel exercises at least three to four times per day to strengthen their pubococcygeal muscle. This muscle is important to the sexual response during intercourse as well as to maintaining bladder control later on in life. Like any muscle, it can atrophy with age; childbirth and weight gain are big factors in the deterioration of this area.

To practice the Kegel exercise, simply contract the muscles you would contract if you were trying to deliberately interrupt the flow of urine. Work up to 10 to 15 repeats, three times daily. Once you've gotten used to the exercise, it also helps to contract these muscles before sneezing, lifting, or jumping to prevent further weakening.

With these coping skills, you can handle multiple life changes and challenges with grace and maturity.

Guidelines For Good Sex

There are few couples that will settle for a sexless marriage. Lovemaking is a secret language, understood only by the two spouses. The following are some proven methods to guide you and your partner to satisfying sex:

- Establish direct eye-to-eye contact during foreplay and, when possible, during sexual intercourse.

- Wear attire, if any, that will promote romance and sexual arousal.

- Speak "sweet nothings" to each other.

- Have sexual secrets that are pleasurable for both of you and are not shared or told to anyone else.

- Schedule time alone at least two to three times each week.

- Edify each other and boost each other's egos and self-esteem by bragging to your spouse about how good a lover they are. Remember that Romans 4:17(b) (KJV) tells us about the power of God when it states; "God, who quickeneth the dead, and calleth those things which be not as though they were." During the sexual experience, keep reaching toward mutual goals with your spouse, keep practicing and praying. New life can come to "dry bones" sayeth the Lord God (Ezekiel 37:1-14 KJV).

- Avoid experiences or discussions that produce anxiety and tension prior to lovemaking so that there can be the best possibility of achieving and sustaining a healthy climax.

- Learn what delays and hastens each other's climaxes and orgasms. It may be withdrawal of the penis to delay the response, for example.

- Honor and respect the fact that men often have their healthiest erection upon first awakening from sleep. This may be one of the best times to engage in lovemaking.

- Women, learn the sports that your husband loves and enjoy the game with him. You might be surprised how passionate he can be after a good game!

- Never compare your present spouse to former lovers or spouses. This is a new day.

- Substance abuse, diabetes, heart conditions, erectile dysfunction and other problems of impotence for men as well as menopause and depression for women are common occurrences in life. Face it, treat it, handle it, and get on with lovemaking.

- Remember that each couple is different. There are as many different marital styles as there are couples. Each couple must communicate and be honest with each other so that they can walk through life listening to the same rhythm and beat of life—their own song of life. And their marital song should be their favorite sound—the sound made when they are at peace and loving each other as God intended.

Epilogue

The Lesson Of The Cactus Plant

We are convinced that God blessed us with the cactus plant in order to teach us about hope, faith, peace, spirit and wisdom. Let us study some facts known about the cactus.

The cactus is the most easily recognized plant family in this world. There are numerous variations between the individual species of cacti. Water is quickly collected by the cactus roots and stored in thick, expandable stems for the long summer drought. When water is no longer available in the summer, many desert cacti shrubs drop their leaves and become dormant. The cactus pays a price for these water saving adaptations and that price is a slow growth.

Cacti owe their success in the desert to their adaptation. They grow as slowly as ¼ inch annually, and can grow on rocky hill-sides or in barren areas throughout the desert where other plants would never make it. They do this by taking advantage of the lightest rainfall, with strong roots close to the soil surface. Those that grow to maturity can reach heights of 30 to 40 feet.

Like the cactus, there will be periods of growth and periods of regression or dormancy in marriage. But also like the cactus, your marriage can grow even with the barest of resources. We want to encourage you that your marriage can improve, be restored, and grow. God can bring the happiness, security and pleasure back that you imagined! Marriage is ordained by God. He has already equipped each husband and wife with what is needed to succeed in their marriage. We must learn how to adapt to the reality of our marital situation and fully accept the spouse that we con-sented to marry.

The cactus is a proven demonstration of God's love. The cac-tus grows despite its harsh environment. It is a true demonstra-tion of survival in difficult natural life forces and earthly circum-stance. No matter what happens, the cactus survives—without anything like the basic necessities, comforts, or luxuries that we enjoy.

Your marriage may grow more slowly than you desire. But marriage cannot mature at a greater rate than the spiritual levels of both partners. Also remember that circumstances, people, and even spiritual forces may knowingly or unknowingly attempt to destroy the marriage.

Marriages may begin under some unlikely and rocky condi-tions. But you and your spouse can learn how to capture the Word of God and other resources needed to help you live peacefully together, adapt to each other and grow. With the personal trans-formation and renewing of the mind of each spouse, and the added gift of time, your marriage can grow to great heights and be strong. If you didn't get married for the right reasons, or under the best conditions, or did so with weak roots, you can still strengthen your foundation and establish a God-centered mission for your marriage. Remember that with God, all things are possible, even if your marriage and home environment appear harsh, drought-stricken, dormant, destroyed, rocky or dead. Like the cactus plant, if you seek from God hope, faith, a peaceful spirit, discernment and wisdom, He will help each of you become new creatures in Christ with the personal power needed for your marriage to flourish.

Appendix:
Resources and References

The Abolition of Marriage by Maggie Gallagher page 117, Dennis A. Ahlburg and Carol J. DeVita, *"New Realities of the American Family,"* Population Bulletin 47, No. 2 (August 1992): 15.

Barna Research Group. (No Date). *(Family)*. [On-line]. Available: http://PageCategory.asp. [March 12, 2001]

Berman, Jennifer. (No Date). *FAQs on Female Sexual Dysfunction* [On-line]. Available: http://www.msnbc.com/news. [July 11, 2000].

Blankehorn, David, Steve Bayme, and Jean Bethke. *Rebuilding the Nest: A New Commitment to the American Family,* ed. (Milwaukee, WI: Family Service America, c. 1990), 97-98. Cited on page 8 of *The Abolition of Marriage* by Maggie Gallagher.

Clinton, Dr. Tim. *Before a Bad Goodbye*: *How to Turn Your Marriage Around.* Nashville, TN: Word Publishing, 1999.

Hart, Archibald D. *The Hart Report: The Sexual Man.* Grand Rapids, MI: Zondervan Publishing House, 1994.

Kozier, Barbara, and Glenora Lea Erb. *Fundamentals of Nursing: Concepts and Procedures.* Englewood Cliffs, NJ: Prentice-Hall, 1999.

Martin, Teresa Castro and Larry L. Bumpass. "Recent Trends in

Marital Disruption." *Demography 26* (1989): 37-51. Cited on page 5 of *The Abolition of Marriage* by Maggie Gallagher.

Nietzel, M.T. and D.A Bernstein. *Introduction to Clinical Psychology.* Citing Erick H. Erickson on page 38. Englewood Cliffs, NJ: Prentice-Hall, 1987.

Osaigbovo, Rebecca. *Chosen Vessels: Women of Color, Keys to Change.* Detroit, MI: DaBaR Services, 1992.

Osaigbovo, Rebecca. *Movin' On Up: A Woman's Guide Beyond Religion to Spirit-Filled Living.* Detroit, MI: Dabar Publishing, 1997.

Rosenblatt, Stanley, *The Divorce Racket.* City: Nash Publishing, 1969.

Taueg, Cynthia. *Planting Seeds For The Harvest of a Successful Marriage: A Guide For Women.* Lincoln Park, MI: To The Glory of God Ministries, 1995.

Thurman, Chris. *The Lies We Believe.* Nashville, IN: Thomas Nelson Publishers, 1989.

Index

72 Hours Rule 110, 125

A

Abuse
   64, 70, 73, 85, 104, 112, 126, 129
Acceptance
   6, 11, 14, 54, 65, 86, 92, 104,
   112, 136
Adultery 75, 112
Alcohol 70, 75
Arguments 81, 85, 97, 105

B

Behavior
   7, 16, 61, 72, 79, 99, 100, 102
   choosing 81
Biblical Courtship 16, 51
Bills 78, 106
Boredom 52

C

Change 59, 68, 88, 93, 111, 112
   anticipation of 65, 86, 104
   personal 54, 83
   positive 95, 99
Choosing a mate 8, 53
Closed Spirit 96
Commitment 12, 65
   fear of 51, 57, 58
Communication 1, 6, 83
   about intimacy 124, 131
   effective in marriage
      67, 79, 91, 92, 96, 97, 99, 100
   full disclosure 6, 56, 112
   guidelines 85
   lack of 129
   non-verbal 80, 89, 97, 112, 123
   secrets for successful 84, 86
   verbal 80, 81, 89, 92, 97, 112

Conflicts
   resolving 83, 122
Consistency 59, 97, 114, 128
Control 55, 87, 90
   loss of 52
Courtship 11, 12, 49 (see also
      dating)
   Biblical 16, 51
   disclosure during 58
Crime 112
Criticism 81, 82, 85, 86, 92, 94
   accepting 88
Crying 105

D

Dating 10, 12, 13
   Biblical 49
   communication during 6, 8
   in marriage 110
   investment 15, 49, 50
   pleasure 14, 15, 50, 61
   purpose of 11
   stages of 14, 15, 49, 50
Dating scale 13
Differences
   between men and women 89, 91
Disclosure (see *full disclosure*)
Distance 66
Divorce 57, 73
   causes of
      67, 75, 76, 77, 78, 105
Divorce rate 73, 74
Dreams
   acceptance of 55
Drugs 70, 112

E

Education 87
Emotional needs 67, 110

Encouragement 88
Entrapment 52
Expectations 11, 66, 72, 100

F

Faith
   testing of 13
      98, 114, 115
Family 91, 95, 111, 112
   history of 7, 8, 100
Fantasies 68, 124
Fear 52, 56, 110
   of commitment 51, 57, 58
   of marriage 57
Finances 53, 105, 113
Food 70
Forgiveness
      53, 88, 97, 98, 99, 100, 101
Friendships 67, 104, 109, 112
Full disclosure 6, 56, 112

G

G-spot 127
Gambling 70
Givers 69, 70, 71, 72
Goals 55, 91, 112
   acceptable relationship 102
God
   relationship with 52, 55, 56,
      72, 78, 91, 99
God-Centered Marriage 108, 137

H

Home (marital) 56, 104, 111
Humility 58, 114, 115
Humor 88, 97, 110

I

Individuality 96
   maintaining 52
Infidelity 65, 66, 67, 126
Intimacy 52, 66, 110, 121
   communication about 124

female 126
male 124
Intolerance 53
Investment Dating 15, 49, 50

K

Kegel exercises 131

L

Laughter 88
Lifestyles (clashing) 54
Lovemaking 104, 121
   attitude during 122, 123, 127
   frequency of 125
   scheduling 123
   guidelines for successful 124,
      132

M

Marital discord (see also *conflicts*)
   causes of
      6, 10, 11, 49, 67, 92, 93, 94
   resolving 83, 122
Marital Mission 1, 119
Marital soul-esteem 86, 87
Marital vitamins 88
Marriage
   biblically based 55
   communication in
      79, 84, 86, 91, 100
   duties before 59
   emulating model 56
   fear of 57
   happiness in 78, 97
   institution of 5
   maintaining 111
   misconceptions of 51
   roles in 91, 94, 112, 121
Marriage rate 73, 74
Menopause 129
   coping with 131
Misconceptions 51
Money 87, 105, 108, 122
   spending 70

N

Name calling 81
Non-verbal communication 80, 89,
    97, 112, 123

P

Partnership 109
Pleasure Dating 14, 15, 50, 61
Post Traumatic Relationship
    Disorder 57
Prayer 54, 86, 109, 114
Pre-Marital Screening Question-
    naire 17, 49
Premenstrual syndrome (PMS) 130
Psychospirituality 114

Q

Quality time 88, 110

R

Relationships
  enhancing
    2, 6, 51, 52, 89, 109, 114
  ending 59, 73
  past 57
  with God 52, 55, 56, 72,
    78, 91, 99
Relationship Goals
    102, 103, 105, 108
Relaxation 88, 131
Respect
    1, 55, 66, 86, 94, 97, 111, 118
Responsibilities
    1, 94, 112, 119, 122
Roles 94, 112, 121
Romance
    91, 92, 96, 111, 112, 128, 132
Royal Personalites 8
  characteristics of 9, 10

S

Sacrifice
  personal 65, 69, 71, 93

Self-pity 115
Sex (see also *lovemaking, sexual
    intercourse*)
  deviant behavior 71
  importance of 111
Sexual intercourse (see also
    lovemaking) 121, 123
  guidelines for success 132
  problems with 96, 124, 129
Sincerity 61
Sole-Soul Takers 69, 71, 72
Soul-Esteem 86, 87
Spiritual marriage 115
Spirituality 113, 114
Stress 54, 70, 83, 109, 121
Submission
    58, 94, 116, 118, 120
Success
  professional and personal 55

T

Trust 7, 51, 56, 57, 118
Truth 6, 61, 85, 99, 112

V

Values
  clashing 54
    86
Verbal communication 80, 81, 89,
    92, 97, 112
Voice 79, 80, 81, 83, 92

W

Wedding Altar Exercise 62
White lies 61
Words vs. actions 10, 92
Work 71, 88, 121
Worship 1, 109, 119

SETTING RELATIONSHIP GOALS EXERCISE			
IDENTIFIED PROBLEM	IDEAL	ACCEPTABLE	PRIORITY NUMBER

Date of Completion_____ Page___ of _____

Name of Preparer _____

SETTING RELATIONSHIP GOALS EXERCISE			
IDENTIFIED PROBLEM	IDEAL	ACCEPTABLE	PRIORITY NUMBER

Date of Completion_____ Page___ of _____

Name of Preparer _____

SETTING RELATIONSHIP GOALS EXERCISE			
IDENTIFIED PROBLEM	IDEAL	ACCEPTABLE	PRIORITY NUMBER

Date of Completion_____ Page___ of _____

Name of Preparer _____

Share It With Others

Marital Secrets

Dating, Lies, Communication and Sex

Name _____

Address _____

City _____ State _____ Zip Code _____

Day Telephone (_____) _____

Order

	Quantity	
	Price	$15.95/book
	Subtotal	
	Shipping & Handling	$1.50/book
or Express 3 Day Service		$3.50/book
MI residents add 6% sales tax		
	Total	

Method of Payment

❏ Check or Money Order enclosed (make payable to RP Publishing)

❏ Visa   ❏ Mastercard

Acct. No. _____

Exp. _____ Signature _____

Mail this form with payment to: **For faster service:**

RP Publishing   phone: 888.955.5055 or 313.537.1000

17620 West McNichols Road   fax: 313.537.0363

Detroit, Michigan 48235   email: finnerwilliams@aol.com

ORDER ONLINE: WWW.FINNER-WILLIAMS.COM

This book is available at special quantity discounts for bulk purchases for sales promotions, fund-raising, or educational use. Special books or book excerpts can also be created to fit specific needs. Please contact us at 888.955.5055 re-garding quantity discounts.

Please allow 4-6 weeks for U.S. delivery. Can./Int'l orders please allow 6-8 weeks.

This offer is subject to change without notice.